Greeks in Michigan

Discovering the Peoples of Michigan is a series of publications examining the state's rich multicultural heritage. The series makes available an interesting, affordable, and varied collection of books that enables students and lay readers to explore Michigan's ethnic dynamics. A knowledge of the state's rapidly changing multicultural history has far-reaching implications for human relations, education, public policy, and planning. We believe that Discovering the Peoples of Michigan will enhance understanding of the unique contributions that diverse and often unrecognized communities have made to Michigan's history and culture.

Greeks in Michigan

Stavros K. Frangos

Michigan State University Press

East Lansing

♾ The paper used in this publication meets the minimum requirements
of ANSI/NISO Z39.48-1992 (R 1997) (Permanence of Paper)

Michigan State University Press
East Lansing, Michigan 48823-5245

Printed and bound in the United States of America
11 10 09 08 07 06 05 04   1 2 3 4 5 6 7 8 9 10

LIBRARY OF CONGRESS CATALOGING-IN-PUBLICATION DATA
Frangos, Stavros.
Greeks in Michigan / by Stavros K. Frangos.
p. cm.—(Discovering the peoples of Michigan)
Includes bibliographical references and index.
ISBN 0-87013-679-8 (pbk. : alk. paper)
1. Greek Americans—Michigan—History. 2. Greek Americans—Michigan—
Social conditions. 3. Michigan—Ethnic relations. 4. Michigan—Social conditions.
I. Title. II. Series.
F575.G7F73 2004
977.4'004893—dc22
2004015880

Discovering the Peoples of Michigan. The editors wish
to thank the Kellogg Foundation for their generous support.

Cover design by Ariana Grabec-Dingman
Book Design by Sharp Des!gns, Lansing, Michigan

Cover photo: A traditional lamb roast.
Courtesy the Berrien County Historical Association.

Visit Michigan State University Press on the World Wide Web at
www.msupress.msu.edu

To the first generation
of Greek-American historians:

Spyridonos Kotakis, Seraphim G. Canoutas,
Maria S. Economidy, and Diogenes Adallis

May their memory be eternal.

ACKNOWLEDGMENTS

I would like to thank a number of Michigan librarians, historians, and archivists. Gordon L. Olson, city historian at the Grand Rapids Public Library, has always shown me every professional courtesy, as has Rebecca Mayne also of the Grand Rapids Public Library. The late Miss Doris Milliman, the Ypsilanti city historian, was most generous of her time when I visited the Ypsilanti Historical Society with the late Dr. Fotios K. Litsas in 1987. I must thank Mrs. Noel Van Gorden, chief of the Detroit Public Library's Burton Historical Collection. My thanks to Barbara Martin, archivist at the Muskegon County Museum, for helping me sort out the history surrounding the Walker Monument. Rosina Tammy of Eastern Michigan University's archives provided me with a number of photographs and other information related to the statue of Demetrius Ypsilanti. In this same vein I must thank Dr. Janet Langlios, former director of the Folklore Archives at Wayne State University, for providing me with information on the history and dispersal of the Greek-American materials. I must acknowledge the guidance of Polly Grimshaw, former anthropology and folklore graduate librarian at Indiana University (Bloomington), and thank her for answering my endless questions.

I need to thank Dr Andrew T. Kopan for answering my many questions related to early Greek immigration and for reading over this account. My special thanks to Alice Kopan, who is currently president of Orthodox Christian Laity, for discussing recent church history with me in some considerable detail. I certainly must acknowledge Dan Georgakas for sharing his knowledge of the history and society of Greeks in Michigan with me over the years. Since I have asked Charles C. Moskos so many questions over so many years, he must forgive me if, while I acknowledge his constant help, I cannot specifically identify what it was I asked this time that he most certainly helped me on.

Finally, this volume would simply never have seen publication with out the years of dedication and constant support given me by Arthur W. Helweg.

SERIES ACKNOWLEDGMENTS

Discovering the Peoples of Michigan is a series of publications that resulted from the cooperation and effort of many individuals. The people recognized here are not a complete representation, for the list of contributors is too numerous to mention. However, credit must be given to Jeffrey Bonevich, who worked tirelessly with me on contacting people as well as researching and organizing material.

The initial idea for this project came from Mary Erwin, but I must thank Fred Bohm, director of the Michigan State University Press, for seeing the need for this project, for giving it his strong support, and for making publication possible. Also, the tireless efforts of Keith Widder and Elizabeth Demers, senior editors at Michigan State University Press, were vital in bringing DPOM to fruition.

Otto Feinstein and Germaine Strobel of the Michigan Ethnic Heritage Studies Center patiently and willingly provided names for contributors and constantly gave this project their tireless support. Yvonne Lockwood of the Michigan State University Museum has also suggested and advised contributors.

Many of the maps in the series were prepared by Gregory Anderson at the Geographical Information Center (GIS) at Western Michigan University under the directorship of David Dickason. Additional maps have been contributed by Ellen White.

Other authors and organizations provided comments on other aspects of the work. There are many people that were interviewed by the various authors who will remain anonymous. However, they have enabled the story of their group to be told. Unfortunately, their names are not available, but we are grateful for their cooperation.

Most of all, this work is a tribute to the writers who patiently gave their time to write and share their research findings. Their contributions are noted and appreciated. To them goes most of the gratitude.

ARTHUR W. HELWEG, *Series Co-editor*

Contents

Greece and the American Imagination

The influence of Greek culture on Michigan began long before the first Greek arrived. The American settlers of the Old Northwest Territory had definite notions of Greeks and Greek culture. America and its developing society and culture were to be the New Athens, a locale where the resurgence in the values and ideals of classical Greece were to be reborn.

With these presuppositions in mind, the way Greeks arrived and preserved their culture in Michigan has an added dimension not usually encountered by other immigrants to America. The newly arrived Greek immigrants actively attempted to deal with the existing myths about the Greeks, and contributed to a two-way process that evolved in Michigan.

The Greek War of Independence: The 1821 Detroit Press Coverage

Grecian Fever was the term quickly coined in 1821 for the worldwide excitement caused by the Greek Revolution against the Ottoman Empire. This bid for freedom especially captured the imagination of Americans still proud of their own Revolution. The Greek War of Independence occurred when Michigan was one of the most distant of Western frontier outposts. The region was mostly inhabited by wild animals and roving bands of none-too-friendly Native Americans. The entire territory boasted only one town, Detroit, and it had fewer than two thousand inhabitants. Here in this most unlikely of locations, four names in particular deserve to be added to the still incomplete list of American Philhellenes: Sheldon, Reed, Woodward, and Leib.[1]

John P. Sheldon and Ebenezer Reed, editors and publishers of the weekly *Detroit Gazette*, spread the gospel of philhellenism to the buckskin-clad frontiersmen of the Michigan territory.[2] In June 1821 the *Gazette* ran five separate items on the Greek War of Independence. By 9 January 1824 the dispatches on the Greek War of Independence had so incited the local population that the *Detroit Gazette* printed an unsigned letter to the editor urging for the formation of a Thespian Society to raise funds to help the Greeks. The anonymous writer asks,

[M]any cities and villages are contributing to this great object, and why, should Detroit be backward in casting her mite?

In 1827, James Ronaldson Leib, son of a prominent Detroit family, saw to the distribution of relief goods to Greece aboard the ship *Levant.* Young Leib, a recent Harvard graduate, traveled to the Mediterranean, where he met with Greek government officials and other American Philhellenes as he distributed an estimated $8,547.18 worth of supplies. Leib was so appalled by the suffering and poverty of the Greeks that he later wrote to his father, saying, the most wretched Indians he had ever seen in America were better off than the people of Greece.[3]

The first chief judge of the Territory of Michigan, Augustus Brevoort Woodward, an ardent classical scholar, left a lasting legacy to the Michigan style of philhellenism. On 14 July 1825 Woodward advertised the sale of his Michigan properties in the *Detroit Gazette* as follows: I have, for some time, been planning a Town on these tracts, under the name YPSILANTI, in honor of the General distinguished for his services in the cause of Grecian Liberty. It is situated in a high and healthy country, with an atmosphere peculiarly pure, aromatic and salubrious. . . . It contains also elegant positions for mills, with abundance of meadow lands, and that of the very finest quality, is also considerable.[4]

These nineteenth-century American estimates of modern Greeks did not result from extensive personal contact with Greek immigrants. Plays, poems, sermons, speeches, editorials and resolutions in Congress fired up the 'Grecian Fever.'[5] Men such as Sheldon, Reed, Woodward, Leib, and other Grecians of frontier Michigan were either men inspired by classical learning and the ideals expressed by the ancient Greeks or men who understood the meaning of liberty and wished the then struggling Greeks success in their own wholehearted bid for freedom.

The Greek immigrants to Michigan learned to build on these existing notions of Greece, and this myth-making has seen some unusual developments. On 29 August 1928, the American Hellenic Educational Progressive Association, a Greek-American fraternal organization, presented the city of Ypsilanti with a bust of General Demetrius Ypsilanti, the work of the Greek sculptor Christopher Nastos, in pentelic marble.[6] Among the Greeks of Michigan there is a popular legend connected with Demetrius Ypsilanti. It is widely contended that Demetrius

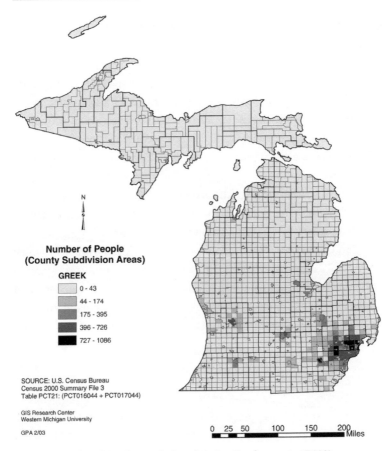

Number of People
(County Subdivision Areas)

GREEK

☐ 0 - 43
▨ 44 - 174
▨ 175 - 395
▨ 396 - 726
■ 727 - 1086

SOURCE: U.S. Census Bureau
Census 2000 Summary File 3
Table PCT21: (PCT016044 + PCT017044)

GIS Research Center
Western Michigan University

GPA 2/03

0   25   50   100   150   200
                                          Miles

Distribution of Michigan's population claiming Greek ancestry (2002).

Ypsilanti not only traveled to America during the struggle for independence but also participated in the Battle of Monmouth on 8 June 1778. The Reverend Harvey C. Colburn cites this legend in his book titled *The Story of Ypsilanti.*[7] Aside from the lack of direct historical evidence for Demetrius Ypsilanti's presence in that famous New Jersey battle, however, the main argument against his physically being in North America is that his father Constantine Ypsilanti was born in 1760, eighteen years before the Battle of Monmouth.[8]

This has done nothing to stop this legend from growing. One recent account not only claims Ypsilanti's presence at the Battle of Monmouth but that he led Greek volunteers into the conflict. While this account goes on to say that there is no record of their origin, the authors are not afraid to postulate that perhaps some of them had come from New Smyrna and St. Augustine.[9] Here the authors are referring to the Greek colonists who in 1768, along with Minorcans and Italians, formed the New Smyrna Colony in eastern Florida.[10] While the existence of these Greek colonists in eastern Florida is an accepted fact of history, however, there is no evidence that they formed a Greek volunteer unit at the Battle of Monmouth.[11]

Only 303 Greek immigrants arrived in America between 1820 and 1880.[12] More may have entered unrecorded or under another ethnic designation. The first Greek is not noted in any Michigan census before 1850, and then only one individual is cited.[13] The number of Greek immigrants to America rose to 183,498 from 1891 to 1910, an increase undeniably attesting to a swift, intentional, and carefully orchestrated migration.[14] Why did these people leave Greece? What role did this massive migration play in establishing Greek communities across Michigan?

Going to the "Ksentia": The Mass Migration, 1891–1921

At the turn of the century Greeks began leaving their homeland in large numbers for the *Kseniti*, (the foreign lands). The decision to labor in foreign lands was most often motivated by a series of social obligations (such as providing a dowry for sisters and acquiring capital in the countryside), by long-established labor practices (verbal and written agreements to work for employers abroad for fixed periods in exchange for the initial fare), by a desire to avoid the growing class discrimination in the rural countryside, and, in the years just before the Balkan Wars and World War I, to avoid military service.

These motivations were and remain commemorated in the folk song tradition known as *tis Ksenitias*.[15] A commercial record copied from a Greek-American living in St. Clair Shores is based on this genre's time-honored tradition.

AFINO YIA (I LEAVE YOU, FAREWELL)
I'm leaving, sweet mama,
And I'm going to foreign lands.

So, give me your hand,
I'll kiss it tenderly and say goodbye.

I ask your blessing and your wish, little mama,
That I make my fortune and return home to you.

So long to my friends, mama,
And to my comrades who revel all night.

So long to my neighborhood, mama,
And to the neighbor-girl that I love.[16]

With that being said, the larger issue of Greek music in Michigan has yet to be fully studied. It is widely recalled that a long-time favorite of many Greek-Americans in Michigan was the rendition of the song Misirlou sung by Maria Karelas Rumell of Detroit. This version was recorded with the Spyros Stamos Orchestra in Chicago on 23 October 1941.[17] Ioannis Halkias, also known as Jack Gregory, was the first musician to record a bouzouki solo anywhere in the world. His Mourmouriko was the introductory theme song of Detroit's *Hellenic Hour*, a daily radio program which ran from the early 1940s until the 1960s.[18]

This out-migration was not limited to America. While reporting on the existence of traditional Greek musical performance outside of Greece and Asia Minor, noted musicologist Sotirios (Sam) Chianis also provides a quick sketch of Greek communities abroad during the period between 1900 and 1930:

By the 1920s there were many Greek emigrants, from both the mainland and islands, in the Congo and Abyssinia and especially in the Egyptian cities of Alexandria, Suez, Port Said, Zazagig, and Ismailia. The majority, however, settled in such cities as New York, Boston, Detroit, Chicago, San Francisco, and Los Angeles. Wherever they settled, these immigrants established strong Greek communities, zealously guarding and perpetuating their religion, language, social customs, and especially their regional folk music and dances. By 1920 each Greek community had several coffeehouses and at least one café-aman, where one could hear (and dance to) live Greek music.[19]

The Greek press, popular journals, and later academics attributed this massive movement to the 1898–1906 failure of the worldwide currant market. The currant grown in the Mediterranean was used in wine making and sought after by the French and Russians to supplement their own grape supply, which had been destroyed by phylloxera insects. With the reestablishment of their own vines, the French and Russians abandoned all currant imports. The long-standing explanation for the mass migrations of Greeks during the period between 1880 and 1920 has thus been directly tied to the collapse of the currant market.[20] The exodus of the first Greeks from the Peloponnesus region of mainland Greece began shortly after this destructive downturn in the national economy.

From a historical perspective, however, the currant crisis is not the only explanation for this mass departure. The Tsintzinians, Greeks from the village of Tsintzina in the heart of the Parnon mountain range east of Sparta, were the first large group to arrive in America from Greece between the early 1870s and the late 1880s. Nearly one thousand young men immigrated from Tsintzina following the nineteenth-century pattern of chain migration to foreign lands to seek temporary employment.[21]

Greeks coming to America clearly saw their migration as a temporary sojourn. The Greeks' expression of their intention was backed by a long history of temporary seasonal and periodic migrations abroad.[22] Accounts left by Greek immigrants who came to Michigan during the 1890s attest to this initial position of high mobility, and accounts of their intentions of staying for only a short time have been gathered from virtually every Michigan community.[23] The commuting of men around the country, the chain migration, and even the later trips back to Greece in the 1930s by entire families can be understood as expressions of this initially tentative commitment to America.

America was simply not the land of every Greek youth's dreams. Almost half of all Greeks who arrived in America during this period returned to Greece.[24] As a group, the Greeks, who, according to the 1940 Bureau of the Census, numbered only thirteenth in total population of the United States, ranked fourth in terms of return rate to their country of origin. Unlike other ethnic groups arriving in America in the late

Members of the Fruit Belt Chapter No. 292 of the AHEPA, ca. 1955. Courtesy the Berrien County Historical Association.

1890s, Greek males outnumbered females two to one, and continued to do so well into the 1950s.

The influx of Greek labor was unacceptable to the average native-born citizen. The establishment in 1922 of the national fraternal organization known as the American Hellenic Educational Progressive Association (AHEPA) was in response to the need to struggle against anti-Greek racism. In 1922 and for a considerable time thereafter, to be a member of AHEPA was not equivalent to being a member of the Elks, Moose, Rotary Club or other service organization. It was like being in the NAACP.[25]

Instead of a community-by-community study I will present those Greeks in Michigan largely ignored in existing accounts and look at some of the major themes of the Greek presence in Michigan. As in all the early Greek communities in America, Greeks in Michigan faced three recurring problems: American hostility over remittances sent back to Greece, Greek immigrants' involvement in European politics, and Greek participation in labor disputes.

The temporary migrant labor position taken by most immigrants especially infuriated native-born Americans. This idea of a temporary sojourn coincided with the invention, in the late 1890s, of the international cashier's check. One of the most often cited problems with the new immigrants was the money, in the form of international money orders, that they sent home. Native-born Americans thought that money earned in America should be spent there. In their eyes, sending money back to Europe drained America of much-needed funds.

In 1911, Greeks in America sent 186,000,000 drachmas (at about 5.18 drachmas per dollar) in remittances to their families in Greece. In 1920 that figure reached 1,191,000,000 drachmas. Naturally this overall pattern of the Greek remittances was not lost on the American economists: Records of outgoing postal money-orders destined for Greece usually show, in comparison with other countries, the highest average amount.[26]

For the Greek immigrants it seemed to be an issue of being in the right place at the right time. For the 1913–1920 period, Mears reports:

[M]ost important of all, however, is the fact that the high level of income in the United States and a period of high prices for confectionary, fruit, restaurant diet, flowers, and shoe-shines, afforded huge savings in America, which were transmitted in large measure for the private economy, largely family savings, and the national economy, largely patriotic loans, of the Kingdom of Greece.[27]

A brief quote from one Michigan newspaper article can offer insights not only into how Greek immigrants provided volunteers for both the Balkan Wars and World War I, but also into the manner in which those who stayed in Michigan actively involved themselves in humanitarian relief work:

A few of the Grand Rapids Greeks have returned home to take a hand in the war as volunteers and more would go if they could. In one way, however, they seem all to be helping the cause at home. They are producing the coin and sending it where [sic] will do the most good in giving the Turks a trouncing. The local banks have been selling more foreign exchange for Greece since the war broke out than in many months before. Owning to the disturbed conditions in the Balkan states the exchange is mostly on London instead of on bankers in Greece. At one of the local banks it is estimated the remittances amount to something like $1,000 a day in amounts of a few dollars up to several hundred. In the banks where the Greeks do most of their banking almost any time small groups of dark complexioned, earnest men can be seen in the corner, and this usually means the purchase of another draft either by an individual or with pooled funds.[28]

One point brought up about Greek economic development is of special interest to our study of the Greeks of Michigan:

> [A]s they prosper they scatter into the smaller cities and towns in order to pursue the few businesses to which they confine themselves, which in turn gives rise to the characteristic feature of Greek immigration—its scattered nature.[29]

The newspaper headlines in Michigan were filled with the daily dispatches from the trenches of first the Balkan Wars and then the First World War. Banner headlines in Detroit, Grand Rapids, and elsewhere reported upon the general turmoil experienced during the period of those two wars. During the Balkan Wars the popular press charged that the immigrants were more concerned with the politics of their country of birth than with America. A number of articles from around the state reported on Greek immigrants in Michigan and their involvement in the war effort at home and abroad. Two especially noteworthy accounts were "Greek Pastor's Daughter Foiled in Attempt to Become War Nurse: Funds for New Church Go across Ocean to Fight Hated Turks," and the impressive *Illustrated Detroit Journal* article, "Greeks Who Returned to Their Country Fight the Turks."[30] Similar articles appeared across the state.

Unfortunately, this essay cannot provide a full discussion of the Michigan Greeks' participation in the sending of remittances to Greece, or a detailed account of their documented involvement in the Balkan Wars and then World War I.[31]

The circumstances and individuals involved in the Greek padrone system in Michigan require us to focus on this issue.

The Padrone System in Michigan

The Greek Padrone System in the United States, is the title of a 1911 Senate Immigration Report that is of great importance for understanding the history and early social organization of Greek communities in Michigan. The padrone system was the systematic exploitation of newly arrived immigrants by their fellow countrymen. This system was neither invented by the Greeks nor exclusive to their ranks. The investigations focusing upon the Greeks as a case study were in no way limited to that group alone: The system at the present time is operated in the United States among Bulgarians, Turks, Macedonians, Greeks, and Mexicans, and among Austrians and Italians.[32] Alciviadis A. Seraphic, a Greek immigrant, submitted this report while employed by the Bureau of Immigration as an immigration inspector. His investigations spanned a period of years and involved his visiting many rural communities, towns, and cities across the United States. This lengthy investigation was prompted by appeals from individual Greeks and community spokesmen across the country. The system worked like this: Padrones (or more often their agents) were paid to bring male immigrants to America. These newly arrived immigrants were not paid a fair wage, were given poor food and housing, were systematically overworked, and were kept from participating in the wider American society. This last point was deemed mandatory by the padrones, so that the new arrivals would not become familiar with the American system and become discontent with their working arrangements and living conditions.

> Among the Greeks the padrone system is in operation in every city of the United States of over 10,000 population, with few exceptions, and is confined in the main to shoe-shining establishments, although it is to a considerable extent prevalent among railroad laborers in the western States and among flower, fruit, and vegetable vendors in Chicago. The aliens utilized by the system in peddling and in shoe-shining are

as a rule from 12 to 17 years of age, while those employed on railroad work are generally adults.[33]

The circumstances of the padrone system still have bitter memories for Greeks around the country. Today, many first- and second-generation Greek-Americans deny such practices ever occurred. Given the reluctance of Greek-Americans to discuss openly these labor practices, few academic accounts address this dimension of Greek immigration to America. The pioneering historian on this facet of the Greek experience in America is Helen Zeese Papanikolas. The career of Leonidas G. Skiliris, the padrone known as the Czar of the Greeks, and his involvement in the railroad and mine strikes in the Inter-Mountain West have received detailed treatment.[34] Regardless of his extensive career and lengthy public involvements in the events leading up to the Bingham Strike of 1912, however, Leonidas G. Skiliris is not mentioned by name in the Senate report on the Greek padrone system.

Padrone Networks in Western Michigan

The 1899 Grand Rapids Business Directory cites a Greek shoeshine parlor where immigrants, then children, worked as part of the nationwide padrone network. The registered owner of this shoeshine parlor was a Peter Smirlis. While I was collecting material for the 1981 National Endowment for the Humanities project that resulted in the museum exhibition *The Greek-American Family: Continuity through Change,* two women in the community, who were daughters of men who had once been shoeshine boys, came forward with information on Smirlis. An immigrant woman and one of the last of the elderly men who had worked for James Talas, Smirlis's partner, later confirmed Peter Smirlis's identity as a padrone during oral history interviews.

The career of Peter Smirlis (spelled Smerlis in the Seraphic report) virtually dominates the coverage in the Bureau of Immigration report on the padrone system. Smerlis is credited with having personally started and operated over 100 establishments in the United States.[35] Rather than just a successful practitioner of the padrone system, Peter

Smirlis was an organizer, leader, and, according to Seraphic's report, principal architect of the Greek padrone system in the New World.

> In the year 1903 Smerlis and some other padrones conceived the idea of organizing a trust of the shoe-shining business in this country and several conferences were held with that end in view. They felt that they could entirely control their labor by having the parents of boys in Greece give mortgages on their property to some representative of the padrones, guaranteeing the time of service of their sons in their employ in the United States. The padrones thought this could be easily accomplished, as it had been tried in individual cases. They proceeded to make arrangements for the consolidation of their interests, but investigations directed by the Bureau of Immigration at this time resulted in the deportation of many boys and gave the padrones the impression that their prosecution was intended under the criminal statutes.[36]

When Smirlis's role in the Grand Rapids community was written into a museum label, local Greek community leaders quickly challenged the identity of this man as the padrone Smerlis. These local Greeks pointed out that the Smerlis cited by Alciviadis A. Seraphic is said to have lived in New Jersey, not Grand Rapids.[37] Seraphic goes on to say that by 1911 Smerlis had sold practically all his places in this country and . . . [was] said to maintain only three in Canada. The *Grand Rapids Press* reported in 1913 that Smirlis was still in the city, as his participation in a lavish full-page newspaper article of that year on local Greek businessmen documents.[38]

While the academic researchers conceded these points, they asked why local Greeks would lie about such a relationship. No answer to this question was ever provided. The community leaders insisted that they be given the names of the local Greeks who had made these claims. When this request was declined on ethical grounds, inclusion of Smirlis's role as a padrone based in Grand Rapids was not allowed in the exhibition. When the community leaders were later pressed by the academic field workers as to why this omission had to occur, since

Smirlis and related padrones had long since left the community, they were simply told, "We have to live here after you are gone."

The local Greeks who contend, to this day, that the Peter Smirlis of their community was the nationally known padrone have never wavered from their claim that he was the man cited in the Bureau of Immigration Report. Peter Smirlis's local partner was a man named James Talas, who gradually bought out all of Smirlis's local holdings. As the 1909–10 investigation took place, oral testimony claims that Smirlis became increasingly distressed and eventually gathered up his family and moved to Canada. The 1913 newspaper article is alleged to have been a media ploy instigated by several local padrones. While certainly not all businesses cited in that newspaper article were members of the padrone cartel, there can be no doubt from the article's tone that the local Greeks felt some positive public relations were needed.

While they protested loudly that the Peter Smirlis of Grand Rapids was not the nationally known padrone, however, in their book entitled *Grand Rapids' Greek Heritage,* Hellenic Horizons, the organizing group from which the museum exhibition sprang, included this amazing quotation:

> Smirlis, who lived in Grand Rapids with his wife Lambrene, is the best known of the city's early Greeks. The operator, according to one record, of over one hundred shoeshine parlors across the United States and Canada, Smirlis was a padrone whose agents in New York City stationed themselves at the docks to ask the young, bewildered debarkees if they had jobs. When the answer was no, the agent would often attach to the boy's shirtfront a tag directing train conductors to send him to Grand Rapids or one of the other cities in which Smirlis operated; the conductors knew Smirlis was good for the fare. Once in the employ of the padrone, the youth was told that he could not leave the boss's service until his passage costs had been paid.[39]

The question is not how cruel or unjust these arrangements were, but how atypical they were for the era in the United States and Greece. This padrone system was known and practiced by other groups, but the

Greeks were among the first to expose this injustice to the U.S. government's immigration authorities.

A strong argument can be made that the forms of labor exploitation employed by the padrone system led to the radicalization of a whole generation of Greek men in America. What was retained, I would argue, was the sense of corporate action. Agnostic relations among the Greeks is a widely held Western stereotype of Greek social interaction. Yet, in many fields of Greek institutional life, including the church, fraternal organizations, and business, they vigorously retained extended networks of service and self-help.

However, the Greeks in Michigan continued to experience a social condition not yet addressed in ethnic studies, with one lone Greek or two extended families representing their ethnic group to an entire small town or rural hamlet.

Greek Communities in Michigan

The Scattered Communities

Written historical accounts of Greek communities in Michigan number only a handful of articles, which often do not provide more than an introduction into the individual community's history. Michigan, Detroit, or Greeks in Michigan are not even listed in the indices of the standard texts on Greek-American history.[40] Collections of random newspaper articles, folklore, and recorded interviews do exist but are cursory accounts and focus only on traditional folk customs and not on the life experiences of the person being interviewed.[41]

The Greek-American ethnic press coupled with available state and federal records indicates that in the first years of mass migration the vast majority of Greeks did not live in Detroit or any other urban area but in predominately rural regions of the state. Oral testimonies gathered among the Greek communities of Michigan confirm this as well. The Reverend Thomas Burgess provides statistical information on Michigan, citing Detroit as having a population of one thousand Greeks, and Other Places having a population of two thousand.[42]

In the section entitled "Scattered Communities," Burgess takes care to stress:

[L]et us remind the reader of that other large and important class of
Greek colonies, or rather of groups of individuals we mean those thousands of Greek men scattered everywhere throughout every state in
the Union, by ones, twos, tens, or even a few more. Such isolated
Greeks, though ever remaining devoted sons of Hellas, become,
because of their very isolation from their fellow countrymen, quickly
assimilated into American life, and are everywhere respected as enterprising business men and good fellows.[43]

From 1907 to 1915 Seraphim Canoutas cited in his annual *Helleno-
Amerikanikos Hodegos: Greek-American Guide and Business Directory*
the names and types of Greek businesses found throughout the United
States and Canada. The intent of these directories was to introduce the
businessmen and suppliers to each other. From our perspective in history these business directories are now invaluable documents. In part
this is due to the fact that Canoutas (and other writers of similar directories) provide us with names of persons and types of livelihood rather
than the mere categories that the various state censuses offer.[44]

In 1911, of the 135 Greek businesses listed by Canoutas in Michigan
only 39 were located in Detroit. For Detroit, Canoutas lists the following businesses: Billiards 3; Restaurants 12; Shoe Shine Parlors 14; then,
under Miscellaneous: Confectioneries 4; Coffeehouses 3; Groceries 2;
and one Hotel. Of the 96 Greek businesses listed for the rest of the state,
11 were in Grand Rapids, 9 were in Sault Saint Marie, 9 were in Jackson,
6 were in Kalamazoo, and 7 were in Battle Creek. Fifty-four other businesses were cited in Michigan (mixed) under the rubric Confectioners,
Fruit, etc.[45]

The Michigan entry in this business directory serves not only as a
rough map of where Greek businesses appeared in the first twenty years
of mass migration but how quickly they dispersed throughout the state
to Adrian, Albion, Alpena, Ann Arbor, Bay City, Bellaire, Cadillac,
Charlevoix, Cheboygan, Calumet, Coldwater, Escanaba, Flint, Glad-
stone, Hancock, Hillsdale, Holland, Houghton, Ionia, Iron Mountain,
Iron Wood, Ishpeming, Lawrion, Lake Linden, Lansing, Manton,
Monroe, Marquette, Mt. Pleasant, Munising, Marionette, Negaunee,
Owosso, Petoskey, Port Huron, Saginaw, St. Johns, and Ypsilanti.[46]

Karagon's Grille was located just north of the Indiana border on U.S. 12 and was owned by the Karagon brothers. Courtesy the Berrien County Historical Association.

Canoutas's 1911 Directory, in comparison to the 1910 Census of the United States, demonstrates the incredibly diverse residency patterns of Greeks in Michigan. Canoutas's citations provide us with individual names, the types of businesses these individuals owned, and even street addresses. One example to illustrate this pattern can be drawn from Grand Rapids: Smerlies, P. 126 Canal, Conf.; Smerlies, P. Monroe, Conf. Smerlies, P. 2 Canal, Sh. We can confirm from this that Smirlis no longer ran a shoe-shine parlor on Monroe Street, as he had in 1899, and that in 1911 he owned three businesses, two confectionary stores and one shoe-shine parlor.

With the 1910 United States Census Report, we can substantiate the Canoutas-Burgess assertion that the majority of Greeks lived and worked in rural Michigan. Comparative work in the future utilizing the various Greek directories and state and federal sources will undoubtedly provide a clearer notion of Greek residency patterns in Michigan. The potential for such a study is clearly evident in a list taken from the 1910 census of the number of Greeks not cited in Canoutas in 1911 and their locations in cities and rural counties of Michigan: 4 in Alger; 19 in Allegan, 6 in Berrien, 2 in Branch, 56 in Calhoun, 5 in Delta, 4 in Dickinson, 1 in Eaton, 6 in Emmet, 34 in Genesee, 2 in Gogebic, 6 in

Grand Traverse, 4 in Gratiot, 30 in Ingham, 3 in Isabella, 31 in Kent, 1 in Lapeer, 13 in Lenawee, 3 in Mackinac, 3 in Macomb, 2 in Mecosta, 7 in Mason, 1 in Manistee, 1 in Midland, 1 in Montcalm, 18 in Muskegon, 1 in Newaygo, 9 in Oakland, 2 in Oceana, 4 in Ottawa, 1 in Presque Isle, 8 in St. Clair, 2 in St. Joseph, 5 in Schoolcraft, 6 in Shiawassee, 3 in Van Buren, and 11 in Washtenaw.

What strategies did the Greeks employ to move so quickly around Michigan? It is safe to surmise that the Greeks actively sought rural locations where they would not face competition. Much of the Greek immigrants' success also can be attributed to the cooperative networks they formed, often over considerable distances.

Greek Networks in Michigan

We do not know enough about Greeks in rural areas to answer the question, What happened when only one individual or one family represented Greeks and Greek civilization to the American community at large? Nor can we ask, What did this social isolation do, emotionally and psychologically, to the lone Greek immigrant or his family members? We do know that the Greeks did not remain alone for long. By the very early 1900s these scattered communities had created a vibrant network of social, business, and religious exchanges and obligations that are still operative today. Business contacts (no doubt enhanced by the Greek business directories) developed into a wider, more informal system of exchanges. Bulk supplies for the Greek immigrants' businesses were supplied by traveling Greek vendors. Trucks from places such as Lansing and Detroit toured the state on both a scheduled and irregular basis, catering to the needs of Greeks all over Michigan.

In addition, the Greek ethnic press in the form of national newspapers and sales catalogues from the large Greek import/export businesses of Detroit, New York, and Chicago brought the isolated Greeks an array of consumer goods through the mail: Greek-language 78 rpm records, religious objects for the home, Greek books, Greek costumes for adults and children, foodstuffs, holiday greeting cards, the services of Greek printers, and even artwork in the form of lithographic prints were just a few of the many items available.

A baptism at the Annunciation Greek Orthodox Church, Benton Harbor. Courtesy the Berrien County Historical Association.

Another tradition, going back to the early 1900s, is the established division of territories within the state of Michigan to specific churches. The parish priest was mandated to travel throughout his territory to attend the remote Greek and Eastern Orthodox families. The various routes covered by these priests are still a time-honored aspect of Greek Orthodoxy in Michigan.

The Greek Communities of the Western Michigan Fruit Belt

From Benton Harbor north along the lakeshore past Muskegon is the fabled fruit belt of western Michigan. While the literature on Greeks in the United States emphatically states that Greek immigrants did not become farmers, many Greeks did in fact own groves in the western Michigan fruit belt. A woman raised on one of the Muskegon fruit groves in the early 1900s recalls that she and her large extended family only infrequently saw other Greeks. All the first cousins of this extended family were taught Greek every Sunday afternoon by an uncle. Church services were held in the family's large rural farmhouse at sunrise. First one of the men would read from the Bible and then a 78 rpm record of Greek Orthodox church music was played on a crank-up Victrola. On holidays special records were played, such as *Kalanda Chrisouyenon* (Christmas Carols), or *Anestasis* for Easter.[47]

Western Michigan had its own regional poet, George Coutoumanos, a member of the Communist Party, who eventually moved from Detroit, due to persecution from U.S. government officials, to Saugatuck. Coutoumanos was renowned as a nature poet who wrote almost exclusively about western Michigan.[48] A section from one of his Greek-language poems, "Indian Summer Imaginings," tells of the beauty surrounding his western Michigan home.[49]

> *Sunrays, burning bright, paint in lavish colors*
> *The wind-lashed Sand Dunes,*
> *Reflecting exotic images beneath the*
> *Balson-fragant banks*
> *Of Saugatuck's Indian-named River*

Communities in Central Michigan

The parish of St. Demetrius Church (physically located in Saginaw) is the center of Greek spiritual and social life for the central part of the state. The parish originally started in 1927 with 35 families, and today has about 125 families. The territory that this church administers includes Alma (1 family), Bay City, Clair (2 families), Frankenmuth (1 family), Gaylord (3 families), Midland, Mount Pleasant (11 families), Saginaw, Traverse City (15 families), and West Branch (6 families). Father Gregory Economiou is a retired priest who served the St. Demetrius community from 1951 to 1975. He once explained the traveling aspect of his ministry to me: "One Saturday, I would go to Mount Pleasant to have a service. Another Saturday, I traveled to Gaylord, another to Traverse City, and so on." These visits were not only a necessary part of the Greeks' spiritual life, they were much anticipated. The Sugar Bowl restaurant in Gaylord is decorated with old photographs documenting Michigan history. Among them are scattered the photographs of Greeks from the central sections of Michigan. Some of these photographs document the traveling church services.[50]

Upper Peninsula

There are two Greek Orthodox Churches in Michigan's Upper Peninsula, at Iron Mountain and Marquette. The one at Iron Mountain claims approximately thirty to forty families. At first the Greek immigrants worked in the copper mines of Marquette and were laborers in Iron Mountain, but gradually they began to open their own small businesses. In both communities, the church community is not exclusively Greek but is also composed of Syrian Orthodox, who now outnumber the Greek parishioners.

The Syrian and Greek Orthodox immigrants banded together not only in the Upper Peninsula but also in Sault Saint Marie, Traverse City, Grand Rapids, and even Detroit. This common bond that began in the Eastern Orthodox Church took a political turn with the 1907 Oriental Exclusion Act. When the immigration of Orientals became restricted in 1907, it was argued that all such persons already in the country should be deported. Given that Syria and Asia Minor were still politically part of the Ottoman Empire, all immigrants from Syria and the Greeks from Asia Minor were labeled Oriental, and so became, momentarily, an unwilling target of this anti-immigration law.[51]

On 10 September 1955, noted folklorist Richard Dorson used a pioneering mechanical device, the tape recorder, for the collection of folk tales. His subsequent article, Tales of a Greek-American Family on Tape, documents the very first instance of extensive recording among Greeks in the Upper Peninsula.[52]

> I drove to Iron Mountain in the Upper Peninsula of Michigan, and
> called on the Corombos family. . . . [F]or eight hours steadily the five
> Coromboses talked to me about . . . Greek matters in the Old Country
> and the United States.[53]

While the family reportedly spoke to Dorson about Greek matters in the United States, we do not learn about them; only the folk tales the family recalled.[54]

Sault Sainte Marie, the coldest spot in the nation, is not a city where one would expect to find Mediterranean people. In 1899, however, the first two Greeks, Jim Poulos and a compatriot named Kostikis, arrived in Sault Saint Marie. In 1900 the Northwestern Leather Company opened a tannery in the Algonquin neighborhood on the west end of Sault Saint Marie, where Greeks were only one of many ethnic groups to arrive for work. In the early 1980s, seventeen Greek families lived in Sault Saint Marie on the United States side, with twice that number on the Canada side. In Ontario the Algoma Steel Corporation drew many of the first Greek immigrants. Through chain migration most of the Greeks living in Sault Saint Marie, Ontario, are from the same village on the Greek Island of Rhodes.[55]

The Greeks of Detroit

Greek immigrants first arrived in Detroit in 1886, with their period of peak migration being from 1911 to 1919.[56] Growth was slow. In 1909 there were a total of 250 Greeks in the city.[57] In 1913, when Henry Ford offered five dollars a day for factory workers, it changed the Greek community overnight. Still there were not more than 8,000 Greeks in Detroit as of 1914.[58] By 1930 the Greeks in Detroit numbered 10,000 to 15,000.[59] Most immigrants hailed from the Peloponnesus region. While no other reliable statistics are available, certainly Greeks from the three islands of Chios, Crete, and Cyprus have always made up a sizeable element of the community.[60]

With its relatively concentrated Greek population and long-established Greektown district, it is not surprising that Detroit also has the distinction of being the location of most academic studies conducted on Greeks in Michigan.[61] The issue of written material on Greeks anywhere in Michigan raises the perennial problem of Greek-American Studies, the failure to have preserved ethnic press publications. Logically one would seek out the Greek-American press for items related to local immigrant or ethnic life and doings within the state. However, I know of no public or private collection that holds extensive Greek press materials (or other documents for that matter) related to the Greek communities of Michigan.

Fortunately, various libraries around the country hold varying runs of *Athenai/The Detroit Athens*. The same is true for the *Ethnikon Vema*

(Detroit Greek Tribune). Both of these newspapers circulated around the United States and would even occasionally carry feature stories on Greek communities in Canada.

Given that Greek ethnic press materials are so difficult to locate, it was simply a matter of luck that I found the 1921 *Panellinikon Hemerologion* (Panhellenic Almanac), with its back-to-back articles "E Elliniki Paroikia Detroit, Mich." (The Greek Colony of Detroit, Mich.) and "Ellino-Amerikana Skitsa: O Pothos tou Yianni" (A Greek-American Sketch: What Yianni Wanted). Written by Savvas Georgias and A. Giamas, these articles are again centered on specific individuals rather than a community history. They provide only a glimpse of the Detroit Greeks before the Second World War.[62]

By 1972, according to the National Centre of Social Research in Athens, there were 100,000 Greeks in Michigan.[63] From the 1890s to the present all available sources agree that the Greek population in Detroit comprises around one-third of the state's total number of Greek-Americans. The Detroit Greektown district has long attracted attention to itself. Little Greece, as this area soon became known, saw its first Greek coffeehouse . . . at the beginning of 1900 at 40 Macomb Street near Randolph.[64] Since 1915, Greek-owned businesses in downtown Detroit have lined Monroe Street. One researcher provides this vivid vignette of Little Greece, as she visited it, in April 1933:

> [T]he . . . district has ten grocery stores, fourteen restaurants, twelve coffee houses, two drugstores, several barbershops, and a general store, which sells almost everything from clothing to icons. Particularly interesting are the grocery stores, which sell exotic wares, where the Greek housewife buys everything needed in the traditional diet. The restaurants on Monroe Street cater almost exclusively to Greek patrons and serve roast lamb and pilaf and other good things included in the fare of all Near East peoples.[65]

In the last forty years many have prophesied the death of the area. To be sure, much has changed, and this district never will be as it once was. Though it has long been recognized as the best-known ethnic region in the Motor City, perhaps the biggest change from the area's beginnings is that today the vast majority of people who visit Greektown aren't Greeks. City and county employees, tourists, business people, and the average citizen can all be found in Detroit's Greektown district.

A survey of businesses, as I saw them in the summer of 2000, can help in understanding the ongoing dynamism in the neighborhood. Today, the Greektown area is comprised of two blocks of businesses, three churches, and a host of the city's municipal buildings. While Monroe Street forms the heart of Greektown, we must quickly point out that not all Greek-owned businesses are to be found on this street. Other streets that are immediately adjacent to Monroe, such as Clinton and Macomb to the north and Lafayette and Fort to the south, also have businesses and buildings owned by local Greek-Americans. Still, the longest uninterrupted stretch of Greek businesses is the two-block run of renovated buildings along Monroe. Randolph Street serves as the westernmost end of Greektown. Without question the slow sweep of the I-375 Chrysler Freeway roughly cordons off the area, which is at the east end of Monroe.

In driving around the district, one is immediately impressed with the number of government buildings that surround Greektown. Detroit's Judicial Center, the Hall of Justice, the old county building, and other such municipal buildings are hand in glove with the Greek-owned restaurants, bakeries, and tavernas. This imposing complex of buildings provides most of the daytime foot traffic trade to Greektown. It is not surprising, then, to learn that while some of the older buildings have been lofted out, few people now call Greektown home. As a judicial and governmental center, Greektown is served by an especially large station for Detroit's mass transit system, the People Mover, to service this complex of buildings. Yet actually hearing someone call it the Greektown Stop can take the unprepared Greek-American unawares. Large signs attest to this designation. This station is located on Beaubien Street right at the corner where it intersects with Monroe on roughly the westernmost end of Greektown.

More than just civic business or a dinner date brings people to this area. Locals recognize the Greektown area as the home to three long-established church communities. As one would expect, to the extreme east of the Greektown area is the Annunciation Greek Orthodox

A Greek wedding inside the Annunciation Greek Orthodox Church, Benton Harbor. Courtesy the Berrien County Historical Association.

Cathedral, at 707 East Lafayette Boulevard. As it happens, St. Mary's Roman Catholic Church, at 646 Monroe, which dates from 1835 and is Detroit's third-oldest parish, is clearly visible from any spot in Greektown. Also within the general area is the Second Baptist Church, at 441 Monroe, which was founded by thirteen former slaves in 1836, and was formerly a stop on the Underground Railroad. On any given Sunday the Greektown businesses see representatives from all three parishes. With urban development and the changes in lifestyles many of these parishioners now must travel many miles to attend the churches. Treasured memories and old family loyalties bring these people to their parishes as much as faith. These are the same things that also quite often bring them to Greektown for an afternoon together.

Detroit's Greektown has its own unique history in terms of public dining and segregation. Sometime during the post–World War II era an unofficial understanding was reached between Detroit's city officials and the Greektown merchants. In the late 1940s and early 1950s the city would send entire juries into the Greektown restaurants, as long as all the jurors were served. No other area restaurants would serve the African-American jurors. Since the Detroit Judicial Center is immediately adjacent to the Greektown district, it came to pass that African-Americans were left untroubled if they decided to eat anywhere along Monroe Street. This de facto desegregation of Greektown not only garnered much good will but also, in effect, acknowledged an accomplished fact.

This sense of Detroit's wider community history is not lost upon the local Greeks. The Greek Merchant's Association, a nonprofit organization loudly declares itself in no uncertain terms to be dedicated to the preservation, advocacy, and education of Detroit's downtown area. Still, the ethnic composition of Greektown has changed significantly, and quickly so. Even in the 1980s all the stores in the district were Greek, with several not particularly interested in serving either the business or the tourist crowds.

As in times past, a representative sample of the Monroe street businesses can be drawn from three typical Greek-owned establishments: restaurants, grocery/bakeries, and tavernas. For restaurants we find the New Parthenon (547 Monroe), with its two-story modernist interior that features Classical Greek statues and numerous murals; the Laikon Café (569 Monroe); New Hellas (583 Monroe), where I was told the lines often extend around the corner on weekends; and the decidedly upscale Pegasus Taverna (558 Monroe). After dinner one may stroll to the Astoria Pastry Shop (541 Monroe) for a Greek coffee and baklava or some other Greek pastry. Combination grocery stores and bakeries can be found at the Athens Grocery/Bakery (527 Monroe) and the Monroe Grocery/Bakery (573 Monroe). To be sure, other restaurants, bars, and shops line Monroe Street. Most prominent among these is the Trappers Alley shopping and entertainment complex immediately next to the Pegasus Taverna.

What may surprise many visitors is that not every restaurant found in Greektown now serves Greek food. The Blue Nile (508 Monroe) is strictly Ethiopian cuisine. The Pizza Papalis Taverna (553 Monroe) features Chicago-style pizza. Fishbone's Rhythm Kitchen is a New Orleans–styled eatery. Furthermore, Greektown has other aspects to it that are far from traditional businesses. The Atheneum Suite Hotel, which is just next to the Fishbone, offers 175 suites to travelers. While the Fishbone and the Atheneum are the innovation of local Greek developers, not everyone is happy with these new introductions.

As a case in point, a once hotly debated introduction to Greektown opened on 10 November 2000: the Chippewa/Sault Indian Casino in Trappers Alley. While the Casino has its main entrance on Lafayette Street, it also prominently features an especially large sign and doorway on Monroe Street. It was Greek-Americans, who were once minority partners in this casino, that first proposed the idea of a casino in Greektown and brought the Amerindian entrepreneurs to the district. Initially local Greeks and other business owners were adamantly opposed to the casino. Yet times change. The MGM Casino, one of the two other casinos in Detroit, earns one million dollars a day. It is projected that the new Greektown casino's daily earning will be two-thirds that number in just the first year of daily operation.

In keeping with the district, the casino's interior features a Grecian thematic décor. Large murals flow across the walls with scenes of rural and classical Greece. In like measure, several of the larger Greek restaurants on Monroe Street are undergoing major renovations to be keep up-to-date with the new casino.

Even in the face of all this change, the Greeks are working together to preserve what they have in Greektown. For example, the Greek Merchant's Association holds three different fundraisers throughout the calendar year. These events always draw the businessmen together as well as bring the community to the district. First comes the Greektown Glendi at the International Conference Center. As one would expect, food, music, and of course belly dancing are to be found. This Greektown event, as with the others, is essentially a food fair, as well as an occasion where money is raised for charity. Old priorities determine when the Glendi is held, since it always follows Orthodox Easter.

Next comes the annual Greektown Art Festival, which is held on the third weekend in May. Monroe Street is closed, and over one hundred artists set up booths on the cordoned throughway. Music is also part of the event, with individual performers and bands playing for the entertainment of all. The Harvest Festival marks the fall season. As in all of these events, food, wine, and entertainment are the order of the day. What sets this event apart is the much-awaited grape-stomping contest. Money raised during this competition is earmarked for the Children's Hospital.

Many local Greeks, who remember a far different sort of Greektown, decry the changes and commercialization of the district. Yet few would move from their spacious suburban homes back to the district, even if they could afford the cost of a loft!

In the early 1900s, Detroit's Greektown served as something of a decompression chamber for the newly arrived immigrants. In the year 2000 the district serves as something more than a physical testament to the business savvy and hard work of prior generations. The image Americans hold of things Greek is what makes Detroit's Greektown work, and that symbolic capital is worth far more to the local Greek community than money alone can ever buy.

This symbolic dimension cannot be overemphasized. In Michigan today, for all the dynamism and change, local traditions often have deep Hellenic roots. In any survey of Greeks in the United States we must always be aware that native-born Americans often unknowingly maintain traditions that were either first initiated by Greeks or are based on local notions of Greek culture. These Hellenic ideas and observances of the past often become a vehicle by which new meanings and social connections are made possible.

Public Presentations of Ethnicity

Classical Greek Performances

The Greeks in Michigan benefited from the experiences of Greek communities around the country that had discovered the benefits of hosting classical Greek dramas and musical performances. The Greeks took care to hold these public events on American holidays, such as Washington's Birthday and the Fourth of July. In the years between 1920 and 1940, every Greek community, hamlet, and family cluster in Michigan had its drama group, playwright, or aspiring opera singer. All reports agree that these public bilingual performances were meant to draw in the American public. One woman from Ann Arbor recalls these events with zest: "[W]e gave plays. We were the actors, the producers, the directors, the costume makers . . . everything! Those were the good old days."[66]

That the Greeks sought to incorporate American perceptions of high art into their performances is demonstrated, in the late 1920s to early 1930s, by a dance troupe from Grand Rapids. Performances were held annually at the local auditorium's Festival of Nations and at the State Fair. These young women would dress in Queen Amalia costumes and perform the traditional circle dances of Greece: the *kalamatiano* and the *syrto*. After this first set of dances, one, sometimes two, of the women would sing the Greek operetta *O Yero Demos* (Old man Demos). Then these same young women would don gauzy white costumes and perform Greek Suites of ancient classical dances inspired by Isadora Duncan's free interpretation of classical Greek dances as they were seen on vases at the British Museum. These dances were the rage in the Roaring Twenties among the upper classes. Not everyone, however, cared for these free interpretations of classical dance. Edna St. Vincent Millay, writing under the pseudonym Nancy Boyd, said:

> I am tired of the Greek dance. I am tired of a group of respectable young women garbed in pastel shades of home-dyed cheese-cloth, limping discretely about in reticent abandon, to the tune of something or other in three-four time. I am tired of the curved elbow, the dangling hand, the lifted knee, the thrown-back head, the parted mouth, the inarticulate bust restrained by a bath-cord . . . the look that registers horror, the look that registers woe, the look that registers that spring is here. . . . Why is it the girls of so many of our best families, the hope of our land, as you might say, insist upon getting all safety-pinned up into several yards of mosquito-netting . . . [and then are found] . . . standing around somebody's golf-links.[67]

What is particularly striking about these ancient dance suites is that the Greek-American young women took part in them at all. The immigrant fathers of these young ladies were exceedingly strict and conservative in the upbringing of their daughters. The publicly presented version of Greek culture and dance, however, apparently outweighed the fact that their daughters were dancing on stage in flowing wisps of white cheesecloth. This sort of dancing was far different from the Greek dancing one could see at public coffeehouses during this same period:

> [I]n large cities like Chicago, Detroit, St. Louis, where there are large colonies of Balkan immigrants, there are coffeehouses for the different strata of immigrant societydingy places for the menial workers and luxuriously appointed parlors that cater to the intelligentsia and the business class. A coffeehouse is generally located in a big hall either

on the first or second floor of a building. It is furnished with marbled-topped tables and chairs with wire-twisted legs. . . . [A]t the back of the hall there is a small kitchen where the proprietor brews the coffee and the tea which he himself serves to his patrons. Lokum, baklava, and other Oriental delicacies are also served, in addition to bottled American soft drinks. . . .

The *kyotchek* troupe [the belly dance ensemble appearing in these coffeehouses] consists of two girls and three men, the latter making the orchestra of a violin, a clarinet and a xylophone. The girls, mostly American born, schooled by the managers to sing obscene Turkish and Greek songs and to dance the sensuous *kyotchek,* are generally plump of bodya discernment on the part of the producers, they having taken into consideration the tastes of the patrons. . . . The troupes now form in Chicago and first present themselves to the critical eyes of the Chicago Greeks. If the girls can do their stuff and meet the approval of the blasé Chicago first-nighters they are instantly booked for long periods . . . with contracts for extended and profitable visits to Detroit . . . and other Midwest cities.[68]

Collective celebrations and entertainments among the Greeks in Michigan were far different than those they offered to the Americans or those enjoyed by the overwhelmingly male nightclub crowd. As one prolific and important Greek-American writer, Dan Georgakas, a native of Detroit, recalls:

[O]ur most spectacular social event was the annual summer picnic held at a campsite rented for the day by father's regional society. For the afternoon, a bit of Michigan became Greece. Lamb and kid would turn on spit, and picnic tables were loaded with gargantuan country salads. . . . Later, tray after tray of pastry would appear, and we would smell Greek coffee being brewed. . . . The only concession to America were soda pop or the kids and a softball game on a baseball diamond to the edge of the park. The center of attraction was the Toledo Five, a quintet comprised of old-county musicians. . . . Their leader specialized in the clarinet and the others played fiddles rather than *bouzoukis,* with sporadic employment of tambourines, flutes, and

The traditional lamb roast is the focal point in all Greek gatherings. Courtesy the Berrien County Historical Association.

goat hide bagpipes. They produced a wild mountain sound that had a thrilling piercing quality. As the retsina and ouzo consumption mounted, the dancing grew more vigorous. There were spectacular leaps and movements by men who momentarily regained the vigor of their prime years. By nightfall, the smells from the food and the sound of the music became magical. Some of the old ballads were so moving they generated communal singing.[69]

The collective celebrations of the Greeks in Michigan have evolved in totally unexpected ways. Some aspects of these changes merit closer attention.

Foodways and the Transformations in Ethnicity

Without question the most commonly held stereotype of Greeks in North America centers around food. While the *Saturday Night Live* routine of cigarette-smoking Greek grill men shouting "cheeseburger, cheeseburger, cheeseburger" may best encapsulate the popular culture association of Greeks with American restaurants, in everyday life it is the Greek festival or bake sale that is most anticipated and attended. In Michigan the single largest event for the majority of Greek Orthodox Church parishes is their annual Hellenic Festival. So protective are the Greeks in Michigan of not just this event but even its very name that they have threatened court action against more than one college fraternity for attempting to host events using, in any combination, the words Greek, Hellenic, and Festival.

This direct association of Greeks with food is not limited simply to popular culture. Significantly, the only subject the Grand Rapids Public Museum staff requested be discussed, when topics for the public programs were being drawn up for the Museum exhibition *The Greek-American Family: Continuity through Change,* was foodways. Even in the preparations for this volume it was suggested that recipes and other discussions of Greek foodways be included. Why has food become a social marker for Greeks? It is far too simple to claim this is just another example of gastronomic ethnics. Rather, it is more interesting to ask questions about the selection of traditions and especially the historical elaboration of the roles of Greek men and women in Michigan.

Let us take one community and see how the ongoing interactions with the wider American community have both reinforced and transformed Greek notions. Since the mid-1950s, the facet of Greek life in Grand Rapids that has received more attention in the local press than any other is the annual *Philoptochos* (Friends of the poor) bake sale. This society is composed solely of the adult women of the Holy Trinity parish. While the *Philoptochos* has long involved itself in local and national civic and charity work, it is its foodways, in the form of breads and pastries, that still predominates as the most publicly identifiable element of the Grand Rapids Greek cultural life.

As in other Greek communities, not just in Grand Rapids but across the country, today the most public contexts for the Greek community events all center around food: dinner-dances, the Calder Festival, the Hellenic Festival, and the annual *Philoptochos* bake sale. Moreover, women, acting as both individual specialists and as a collective, have

The Annunciation Greek Orthodox Church Philoptochos displaying their baked goods, probably for a Greek picnic, ca. 1965. Courtesy the Berrien County Historical Association.

moved out of their private kitchens to offer their pastries to the community at large. Food, then, has become a public medium for presenting Greekness to the American public. The symbolic importance in Greek culture of food and hospitality has shaped the way Greek-Americans understand their own actions. *Philoksenia,* (hospitality extended to strangers) is the explanatory term Grand Rapids Greeks use to describe the obvious zest with which they apply themselves to their food events.

The food management skills learned at home festivities, in family restaurants, and over the years of presenting community events have resulted in a virtual science of hospitality. It should be stressed that the enthusiastic response of the American community to these bakery goods has also reinforced certain rural Greek values about women. While at the same time that the large-scale public preparation of food has progressively brought women out of their traditional domain of the home it has simultaneously strengthened Greek notions of femininity and nurturing. In Grand Rapids the women proudly proclaim that this ability to prepare food comes from their training in the home as good *nikokyres,* literally good homemakers.

Finally, while in the past two or three families managed community dinner-dances, today these (admittedly larger) events utilize the entire community in a highly sophisticated food management situation where literally hundreds of pounds of food are prepared and thousands of dollars are made. It is no secret within the Greek-American community at large that the development of the now-colossal food festivals and bake sales has provided the financial means to build the huge new church complexes one sees all across the United States. No community of less than two hundred families, such as that in Grand Rapids, could afford the imposing church buildings it now possesses without the monies generated by the highly successful festivals and bake sales. This last point cannot be overstressed, for there is more at stake than the mere expansion of the once largely private church picnics into the decidedly public Hellenic Festivals. As the demography of Greek America slowly declines, there are not only fewer parishioners at church but also fewer still to work at the festivals, a point not lost upon Greek-Americans.

We would be remiss in our discussion of the selection and process of ethnicity if the American response to traditional food was overlooked. In response to American tastes, *stefado* (a wild meat dish, usually rabbit or a game bird, with onions and cinnamon as the principal spice), a main dish of the 1930s dinner-dances, has been replaced by dishes such as *shish kebab* or *mousaka.* Also, Greek peasant main dishes, such as village-style salad; the combination of feta cheese, olives, and bread; or *dolmades* (rice and spices wrapped in a cabbage or grape leaf) are now (in a more affluent America) side dishes. The ingredients of all the traditional pastries are far richer (more eggs, butter, and sugar), and include items not traditional to rural Greece (such as ricotta cheese, frozen spinach, and so on), and many dishes are also now prepared with a more diverse combination of ingredients, as in the combination of four or five cheeses in one dish.

Food is a very telling example of how past regional distinctions among Greeks have now merged. A typical Greek-American dinner in Grand Rapids can combine regional foods in a manner never possible in either rural Greece or in the early days of this Michigan community. For example, a dinner can now include *pastichio* (a dish found all over Greece but with various possible combinations of ingredients, such as ground beef or fish, that are interchangeable), black olives (Kalamata region), feta, village salads, and pastries like *bereki* or *pishia* (both from the Black Sea area of Asia Minor).

As we have seen, the American phenomena of a dinner-dances or bake sales has marked a time of commensality when individuals, ethnic and American alike, have met and learned about each other. A major shift for the Greek immigrants is the movement away from ritual events signaling an occasion when only Greeks (and perhaps a few close American friends) would gather to share food (for example, name days, baptisms, weddings, and so on) to progressively more secular events (such as dinner-dances, bake sales, and the Calder Festival). This movement has also signaled a transformation in celebratory space away from small, intracommunity gatherings to public celebrations encompassing all of Grand Rapids. Photographs offer the thoughtful viewer unexpected insights into the changing relationships within the Greek-American family since the time of the 1880 to 1920 migration.

Picturing the Greeks in Michigan

The precise role and social function of photography in Greek-American life has never been systematically studied. Much can be learned, however, about how Greeks interact with the social worlds in which they find themselves by studying the photographs Greek-Americans take and ultimately choose to keep. The historical changes evident in Greek-American photograph collections mirror the transformations in these people's daily lives.

Few Greeks realize that daguerreotype photographers were present in Greece little more than two months after the camera's invention in January 1839. Noel Paymal Lerebours (1807–73), a French publisher, was the first to realize the potential profits from illustrated travel books. In

The Couvelis family ca. 1930. Courtesy the Berrien County Historical Association.

March 1839, Lerebours sent a group of photographers to take the very first photographs of Classical Greek monuments.[70]

By 1847, Filippos Margaritis had become the first documented Greek photographer. The East Façade of the Propylaea is Margaritis's first known daguerreotype. Other Greek photographers quickly established studios throughout the Balkans and eastern Levant. Many Greek families all over the world own daguerreotypes, albumen prints, calotypes, and cabinet-card photographs taken of their relatives by photographers in Athens, Constantinople, Smyrna, Alexandria, Jerusalem, Thessaloniki, and elsewhere.

Fieldwork conducted in Michigan shows that many of these early cabinet-card photographs are to be found in Greek family albums. The early Greek immigrants were far from passive subjects before the studio photographer's lens. Photographic traditions inspired by the Greek-

American experience can still be seen proudly displayed in many homes. At the very start we must be careful to distinguish between photographs taken by Greek-Americans and those that they commissioned. Greek immigrants arrived in North America just as photography became a relatively inexpensive consumer item. Since initially few could afford to own a camera, studio photographers were sought out for special events. Among the Greeks in Michigan it is clear that very specific types of photographs were sought, and for very specific reasons. As we shall see, at the heart of all of these photographs were notions about the family. Let us review two very specific genres of early Greek immigrant photography and then see how those very same images are regarded today.[71]

Composite Photographs

Across Michigan, from one Greek-American community to another, one will effortlessly find among the very oldest of family portraits those that have come to be called composite photographs.[72] Combining the negatives of two or more separate photographs makes a composite photograph. The persons appearing in these photographs are reduced and rearranged in the studio darkroom to create the semblance of a group portrait. The Greeks did not invent this technique. Such collective composite images were a common practice first made popular by Victorian studio photographers.

The widespread use of composite photography across Greek America, not just among the Greek communities of Michigan, chronicles the fragmentation of the Greek family. Separated by immigration, wars, and even death, it was often only in photographs that the family gathered side-by-side. We should quickly note that individuals could also be photographically removed, signaling a rupture in the family. Given the skill of the studio photographer involved, some of these portraits are nearly flawless images. At other times the blurry images and startling incongruity in relative body sizes in these composite photographs is striking, yet this is rarely commented upon by the owners of such photos. However crude some of these portraits may be, they were for the immigrant visual statements of a desired, rather than actual, family unity.

With this being said, that does not mean the available photographs cannot serve as evidence for other sensibilities. A photograph of the Anchaclis wedding party, like many early photographs found in Michigan and elsewhere in the country, shows a wall-to-wall hanging of photographs that literally covered nearly every square inch of space, which was common decorative motif of Greek immigrant households during this era. This employment of embellishment is seen in other Greek settings as well. Among the Sarakatsani, wandering Greek herds-men, the interiors of their animal tents are decorated by continuous pieces of embroidery that begin and end at the tents' openings. In Greek island homes of the Dodekanese Islands at the turn of the cen-tury, the interior walls were lined with photographs, hand-painted plates, and lithographs. In all three settings the interior space of the home was literally lined by the social world that those who lived in that residence allowed in.

What is also interesting to note is that many prized family photo-graphic keepsakes were originally the special extras offered by the pho-tographer, rather than the initial commissioned portrait. As a means of drawing customers to their studios, many enterprising professional pho-. tographers offered a selection of extra prints. Rather than offering, say, a mere selection of different sized extra prints, these professional photog-raphers would instead offer, along with the large formal portrait, several prints on postcards, copies of the photograph on oval metal plates, or even a print of the photograph on one side with a mirror on the other.

A major problem, however, with discussing the photographs of the Michigan Greeks is that those images were not always taken in the state, and often they did not stay in the state very long. A photograph that can be found in a number of family collections in Midland, Michigan, and, as we shall see, elsewhere as well can serve as an example.

In the spring of 1922 Anastacia (Tasia) Rapanos arrived in Chicago, Illinois, from her home village of Planeterou in the Kalavryta District of the Peloponnesus. Upon her arrival, Tasia went to live with her four brothers, Athanacios (Tom), Alexandros (Alex), Haralambos (Harry), and Spiro (Sam). The family was then living in a small apartment on Dewey Street. At a stable nearby the brothers kept at least two wagons, from which they sold fruits and vegetables. Rather than continue sending their clothes out to the laundry, Tasia pocketed the money the brothers gave her and did the cleaning and ironing herself.

Sometime between 1922 and 1924, Tasia Rapanos commissioned a family portrait of herself and her brothers Alexandros (Alex) and Athanacios (Tom). By the time she had saved enough for this portrait photograph, many things had changed. Most conspicuously, Spiro and Harry had moved out of the Dewey Street apartment. The newly established social relations in America between Tasia and the various brothers can be seen in the fact that only Tasia, Alex, and Tom are shown in this composite photograph. While the exclusion of Spiro and Harry might be interpreted as an example of severed family ties, however, the contemporary use of this photograph, in its several forms, is quite the reverse. This picture is now used by descendants of these three individuals to express their unity.

The copies of this formal portrait no longer simply represent images of one's family or love of one's brothers. They are not even merely photographs of one's father or grandfather alone. This composite photograph now serves other social purposes. For example, this photograph is now the mnemonic cue for very specific stories about family immigration. Interestingly, not all the same stories are recalled; it depends upon who is telling the story. Thus, today no one copy of this photograph is recognized as the original.

Alex eventually married and moved to Midland, Michigan, where various members of his extended family, including two of his three sons and their families, still live. Among these family members, small, postcard-size versions of the composite portrait can be found with various information written on the back. The separate photograph showing just Alex, which was used to make the original composite portrait, was given by one of his sons to a brother now living in Naples, Florida. In the stories told about both the giving and the receiving of this photograph it is clear that men not used to expressing their affection for each other found a source for this emotion through this photograph.

One of Tasia's grandsons, who lives in northern Illinois, sent a copy of the composite photograph, as it appears on an oval hand-held mirror, to a grandson of Tom's who now lives in Laconner, Washington. Thus, this single photograph continues to link relatives over long distances.

Death Photographs

In the long years of separation between immigrants and family back in Greece, death was all too frequent. When possible, funeral photographs were taken on both sides of the Atlantic. In Michigan they were the last images of a loved one. In Greece they proved to the grieving that the deceased had been buried according to Eastern Orthodox Church ritual. Sometimes, in moments of great disaster, such as the 1918–19 swine flu epidemic or the holocaust of the 1922 Asia Minor Catastrophe, it was simply impossible to take commemorative photographs. At those times immigrants frequently chose some other photograph of the lost relative that through stories became the signifying image of the loved one's death.

Sometimes a funeral or death photograph propels the speaker into a whole narrative about the people seen within the frame of this one image. A series of photographs from a family in Muskegon Michigan can help illustrate this sort of narrative event.

Regrettably, it is now often the case that for the entire generation that came to America in the 1870 to 1920 era, only one or at the most two people in an extended family remain alive who can identify all the individuals one sees in the old pictures. For the Bilderyadis and Eustathion families, Anne Eustathion Kekatos is such a person. Anne is now the oldest living member of both her father's and her mother's families. She is the final source for identifying scores of family photographs. In the course of discussing a funeral photograph, Anne Kekatos soon began referring to people, events, and other photographs spanning nearly a hundred years and several continents.

In the summer of 1921, Anne's strong-willed grandmother, Anika, and mother, Penelope Bilderyadis, arrived in Muskegon, Michigan. The two women had journeyed all the way from the sizable town of Saranta Ekklesia in eastern Thrace, then a part of the Ottoman Empire, to see their daughter and sister Chryssie. Unexpected tragedy awaited the women. Chryssie had died of diabetes literally just before their arrival. A photograph had been expressly taken of the Chryssie's burial, because with Anika and Penelope in transit, there was no way they could attend the funeral. At the graveside one can see her husband, Sarando (Sam) Anchaclis; his only child with Chryssie, Bea (Panayota); and other family members.

While the family was still collectively recovering from Chryssie's death, photographs by a professional studio photographer were sought out. In one, Penelope, Sam Anchaclis, and Bea are shown in their Sunday dress finest. This perhaps unexpected act requires some discussion. Greek-American photographs have always been used to showcase and present the family. Therefore, this kind of photograph indicates an affirmation of family unity rather than any disrespect for the dead. Other things about this story, though, are far from certain.

Why exactly Anika and Penelope came to America has never been determined. In typical Greek fashion, several versions are told about the same event. Most often the idea that the two women were just coming for a visit is presented. Yet other information seems to contradict this claim. To begin with, the two women used the name Bilderyadis on their passports. Bilderyadis was Anika's maiden name. In America the large Bilderyadis clan had shortened its name to Bilder, and the two women followed suit.

As with many Greek families from this era, the separation of continents also meant differences in the times when one was married. Thus while brothers and sisters were not far apart in age, the children they would eventually have in America were often widely separated by age. In the case of Penelope Bilder, she had one first cousin, Helen, and a niece, Bea, who were only about ten years her junior. These two women proved an important bridge for their female relatives who were to be born after them.

To this day Anne refers to her late cousin only as Doctor Helen. Helen Bilder was one of the very first women from Chicago's Greek community to become a medical doctor. Bea eventually became an extremely wealthy businesswoman in Burlington, Vermont. It was Bea who approached Penelope, Dr. Helen, Helen's mother Athena, and other women from Saranta Ekklesia, time and again, to find out why her grandmother Anika came to the United States and why she used her maiden name. Bea never learned anything for certain, but she did know enough to tell her first cousin, Anne Eustathion Kekatos, that they were hiding something.

Loss of social status certainly seemed part of the mystery. In part this can be judged by some of the family's oldest photographs. The much-loved photograph of Great-Grandmother Chryssie with her three grandchildren reveals the three children in less than expensive clothes. Tom, in fact, has no shoes. No mention was ever made of Anika's husband, not even his name. All that was left behind in the mountains of Thrace. The bond between Anika and her children, then the cousins, especially the women, remained strong.

According to Anika and Penelope, life and people in the town of Saranta Ekklisses were sophisticated, not like, these two women always contended, the manners and actions of the Greek rural villagers one found in Ameriki. Some of this sophistication can be seen in the photographs of Anika's sister Elenco. Many of the Elenco photographs are expensive studio portraits, which always present her in a refined setting. Two images in particular are especially interesting because they are cabinet card photographs taken by the same local photographer, C. Zafiriades. While each of these photographs is worn due to much handling, the two names of their hometown, Saranta Ekklesia and Kirk Kilisse (the official Ottoman name for this town), are visible on the photographs.

The changes in the roles and self-images possible for Greek-American women can be seen as we compare Elenco Bilderyadis's photographs with those of the young women born in America to immigrants who hailed from Saranta Ekklesia. To see the social and cultural distance the older people traveled, one need only compare Elenco's neck-to-ankle dresses with the one-piece bathing suits worn by the young people of Anne Kekatos's generation in other photographs in her collection.

Anne frets sometimes because a number of the oldest photographs are damaged. This is not due to any kind of disregard. Quite the opposite. Penelope handled them so much as she aged that some photographs literally have their corners worn off. Anyone who has studied Greek-American photographs of the immigration generation will know that this is far from unusual. Broken corners, split photographs, attached labels, and writing on the front and back of the photographs all regularly occur. Members of the preceding generations have been as engaged with their past experiences as we are with our own. It is more than a question of our common humanity. The Greek immigrants who came to America between 1870 and 1924 arrived just as the camera became a cheap consumer item. As advertising taught native-born Americans how to have a Kodak moment, it also taught the newly arriving immigrants the manner in which to use this new technology.

As with the Rapanos composite photograph, the images of the Bilderyadis/Eustathion family are now scattered across the United States. Anne Kekatos has provided copies, and even some original family photographs, to relatives in Burlington, Vermont; Oak Park, Illinois; and Mobile, Alabama.

While I was able to interview a number of the original Michigan Greek pioneers from the 1870 to 1920 wave of immigration, the majority of the fieldwork I conducted was with individuals one or more generations removed from the person or persons who first commissioned or took the photographs we examined together. This distinction is critical. The meanings of these photographs are therefore interpreted from the perspectives, memories, and experiences of children or even grandchildren of the original immigrants. The immigration history drawn from such sources is often abbreviated. What does come to the fore is how the social and historical meanings of these photographs have continued to accrue rather than collapse into one repeated formulaic explanation. Thus while immigrant-era photographs continue to link families across great distances, their symbolic meanings are now of a different order of experience and must be understood as such.

The Man with the Branded Hand

As the case of the Walker Monument in Muskegon documents, the ongoing relationship between Greek immigrants and the life and landscape of the peoples of Michigan is quite complex, with Old World experiences holding great influence over the actions of daily life among these immigrants.

In 1799, Jonathan Walker was born on a farm in Harwich, Massachusetts. Walker, who took to the sea as a young man, became both a sea captain and a committed abolitionist. Like many more abolitionists that are now recognized, Walker actively helped African American slaves escape their bondage. In 1844, while making a voyage from Key West to the Bahamas with seven fleeing slaves, Walker's ship was overtaken by the sloop *Catherine* and captured. He was tried, convicted, and sentenced for stealing slaves. Walker was placed in the pillory (where he was pelted with rotten vegetables and eggs), branded with a red hot iron on the right hand with the initials S.S., signifying slave stealer, sentenced to a year in jail, and forced to pay a fine of six hundred dollars plus the cost of prosecution. Since Walker was tried before the Superior Court of Escambia County in West Florida, he has the distinction of being the only person in American history to be branded under a federal court order.

Walker's trial and especially the form his punishment took caused a national sensation. Noted poet John Greenleaf Whittier (1807–1892) composed "The Branded Hand" in honor of Walker. The Quaker poet urged Walker not to be ashamed but rather to hold his hand aloft, for all the North and the world to see:

> *Hold it up before our sunshine, up*
> *Against our Northern air,*
> *Ho! men of Massachusetts, for the*
> *Love of God, look there!*
> *Take it henceforth for your standard,*
> *Like the Bruce's heart of yore,*
> *In the dark strife closing round ye,*
> *Let that hand be seen before!*

In 1863, Walker purchased a few acres of land at Lake Harbor, located in what was then Muskegon County. Walker settled into a peaceful life of working his small orchard. On 30 April 1878, Walker peacefully died. Unfortunately, Walker's relatives were unable to erect a tombstone over the grave in Norton Township cemetery. On learning this, Photius Kavasales Fisk (1807–1890), of Boston, Massachusetts, stepped forward to do so at his personal expense.

Fisk was a retired Congregationalist clergyman who had served as a chaplain in the U.S. Navy. He was also a man who knew about being a slave. Fisk, who had been born Photius Kavasales in the Peloponnesus region of Greece, was raised in Smyrna, which is located along the coast of Asia Minor and was then a part of the Ottoman Empire. With the fall of the city of Constantinople on Tuesday, 29 May 1453, the Byzantine Empire, and all the Greeks within that polity, had been ruled to be slaves of the Ottoman Turks. Freedom for the Greeks was not regained until the Greek War of Independence, 1821–1829. Young Kavasales, as a Greek Christian subject in the Ottoman Empire, was born a slave.

Reverend Pliny Fisk, an American missionary, met Kavasales on the island of Malta while the youth was studying at a Jesuit college. Reverend Fisk convinced the young Greek to continue his education in the United States. Thus began Kavasales's schooling first at Amherst

College and later at Auburn Theological Seminary. Yet the young Greek immigrant never forgot his past. True, in time Kavasales would take the last name of his American missionary benefactor as his own. However, other memories and beliefs were obviously at work in this man's life. Most significantly, this Greek immigrant's long career as a clergyman in the U.S. Navy was not without controversy. This, perhaps, could not have been avoided. As Parker Pillsbury noted at Walker's memorial service in 1878, the young Greek immigrant had become quite too much an abolitionist to be patiently tolerated in an American pulpit. So, aided by such men as John Quincy Adams and Joshua R. Giddings in Congress, and Gerrit Smith and other equally well-known men outside the government, he received (in 1842) the appointment of Chaplin in the United States Navy.

It was Photius Kavasales Fisk who wrote the eyewitness report on flogging aboard U.S. Navy vessels. Once this report was presented to Congress, that body forever banned such practices. Rather than praise him for such an effort, however, the officer class never forgave the Greek-born clergyman for not simply submitting this report but going to Congress and actively lobbying for the ban against all forms of physical discipline within the navy. It was then felt, and quite strongly, that only by the means of flogging was proper conduct aboard ships assured. Soon after his report Fisk was stationed at a navy yard and largely forgotten by the navy until his retirement.

A man of strong faith, Fisk never denied his affiliation with the American abolitionist movement. Furthermore, Fisk did more than simply talk. In Lyman F. Hodge's biography of this remarkable man, we learn of the good chaplin's years of philanthropic work. Many of the most prominent abolitionists died paupers. Having given literally their all to the cause of freedom after the Civil War, many of these dedicated individuals lived a life of poverty, often dying with nothing. As Reverend Fisk learned of such individuals he was determined that their deeds would never be forgotten. So, Fisk paid for the burials and for the placing of imposing monuments over the graves of such persons as the Reverend Charles T. Torrey, Henry C. Wright, William Shreve Bailey, Jonathan Walker, and others.

In Walker's case, Fisk first insisted that the grave be moved from

Norton Township cemetery to Evergreen; the main cemetery for Muskegon. Importing Hallowell granite from Maine, Fisk had an impressive monument created. The four-sided stone obelisk was mounted on a three-section base, which itself was nearly five and a half feet high and three feet square. The base rests half below the ground. The second part of the base, called the plinth, is fully exposed above the ground. Finally, the third section of the base, called the die or dado, separates the base and the shaft. The shaft is six feet high and rises in a taper to a pyramid top. The total height is ten feet five inches and the total weight, two and half tons. The obelisk still stands about a hundred feet from the entry gate of the Evergreen Cemetery.

On the east face of the shaft is the inscription "Captain Walker's Branded Hand." Immediately below these words is a carving of Walker's right hand with the letters S.S. on it set within an oval. On the upper base on the same side is Walkers' full name, along with the dates and locations of his birth and death. On the north side is a brief quotation from Whittier's poem. On the south face is inscribed:

> *This monument is erected*
> *To the Memory of*
> *Capt. Jonathan Walker,*
> *By his anti-slavery friend,*
> *Photius Fisk Chaplin of the*
> *United States Navy*

This monument was dedicated on 1 August 1878, with literally thousands of people in attendance. Yet the story of the Walker Monument does not stop here.

On 8 August 1998, fully 120 years after Walker's death, the monument was restored and rededicated. Another monument—a four-hundred-pound boulder commemorating Walkers' wife Jane—was also part of the ceremony. A family reunion for Walker descendants and their relativesmany of whom met for the first timewas part of the wider cycle of events. Just as with the first dedication ceremony, literally thousands of people attended the rounds of rededication events.

The good Reverend Photius Kavasales Fisk could never have imagined how well his monument to Jonathan Walker would serve its ultimate purpose. Since 1878 thousands of visitors have sought out the inner city Muskegon cemetery for the grave of the Man with the Branded Hand. Today, we can only imagine what it must have meant for a man born into slavery to honor a man who was branded for the act of freeing slaves. We do know that the Walker Monument stands forever as a testimony to the resolve, bravery, and sacrifice of all the American abolitionists.

American-Greek Society in Michigan, 2001 and Beyond

Census figures and daily reality point to the inevitable assimilation of Greeks into the wider American culture. This seemingly undeniable fact has been met with considerable fury. Today, not just in Michigan but all across the country, there are two more or less distinct groups: those who proudly recognize descent from Greek immigrant ancestors but see themselves as principally Americans, and those who contend they are Greeks living abroad. While this opposition of identities is an eternal constant in any ethnic or Diaspora community, at this point in time in North America, specific social and economic factors among the Greeks charge this duality with grave possibilities.

The battleground for this contest is no longer the free-for-all debating space of the coffeehouse of the 1900s but the after-Sunday-service church coffee hour, and the location for the everyday expression of this dispute is the administration of the local community church. As Greeks understand themselves, they differ most markedly from other religious faiths by virtue of the fact that they are simultaneously ethnic Greeks and Eastern Orthodox Christians. The immutability of this identity is due to the centuries of oppression and political rule by the Muslim Turks, and has only been strengthened in an American setting where immigrants and their descendants have made the church, rather than

This painting, entitled Long Live Greece, *shows the connection and love Greek Americans have for their new adopted country as well as their patronage to their old. Courtesy the Berrien County Historical Association.*

any other institutional form, the very center of their identity in the New World. Many have written in the past of how the church in America became the de facto village center for the Greeks. But within the last twenty years much has changed.

The Greek Orthodox Church in North America is now composed of a hierarchy largely from Europe, with an overwhelming majority of parish priests and parishioners born in America. Approximately 80 percent of the marriages that take place within the Greek Orthodox Church are now to non-Greeks. Unfortunately, with the 21 September 1996 enthronement of Metropolitan Spyridon (George Papageorgiou) as the archbishop, the long-simmering debate over the issue of Greek-American assimilation flared up as the pivotal question in Greek Orthodox parishes around the country. While it is said that at the heart of this conflict is the issue of the proper manner in which to expressone's Greek identity and Orthodox faith, more is at play. The subtext to this rancorous debate is clearly who will manage community property and church funds, as well as regulate the daily and cyclical activities of the individual parish. With over 550 established parishes and chapels in the United States generating annual revenues in the millions, much is at stake.

Regrettably, in many parishes around the country litigation was and continues to be the result. Michigan parishes were not excluded from this national controversy. Sophia A. Niarchos's article "Bishop Rejects Civil Court Request for Help" is only the latest in a seemingly endless series of news articles that have documented the difficulties in the St. George parish of Southgate, Michigan.[73] The many Greek-language articles in the *Ethnikos Kirix* (National Herald) out of Astoria, New York, have detailed the legal proceedings in this one parish with almost microscopic attention.

The still-unresolved dispute over church governance and the instigation of legal cases prompted by this ongoing and heated debate can be seen in as many varying degrees from one Michigan parish to another as with the rest of the country.

Interestingly, the wider debate within the Greek Orthodox Church went online, and although the persons responsible and the reasons for the initial controversy have passed from the scene, a special website is still maintained that documents the marked differences of opinion concerning the proper roles of the laity, parish priests, bishops, and hierarchy in North America.[74] With an estimated three thousand articles, statements, letters, speeches, responses, and so on, this website is an invaluable historical resource.

This series of events has generated its own corresponding literature. Sources that relate the historical development of this great divide and see the inevitability of assimilation are the most numerous.[75] Yet these writers have not gone unchallenged. Anna Karpathakis argues for the opposite position, which

on an ideological level [sees] it is a church and religion unique to
Greeks. . . . They see the Greek Orthodox Church as an immigrant
church established by Greek immigrants for the sole purpose of car-
rying on the Greek heritage, language and traditions.[76]

From yet another perspective, Constantine G. Hatzidimitriou, in his
Church-Community Relations in the United States, specifically challenges the demographic argument that Greeks are assimilating into the
broader American society in the fashion alleged by numerous writers.[77]

This debate is a complex and broadly based argument. Aside from
the appropriate role of parishioners within the administration of the
local parish (and who gets to handle parish funds), other issues are regularly discussed. The current debate over the roles of the local parish
laity and the archdiocese inevitably encompasses the pivotal person of
the parish priest. How the very form of the Greek Orthodox Archdiocese
has changed over time to meet the new realities of Greek self-identity
in North America has also seen discussion.[78] The recent installment of
the new Archbishop Demetrius (Trakatellis) has somewhat improved
the general situation, but the long-term outcome is still in question.

The opposite to the assimilationist position is not just cultural
maintenance but Hellenic Renewal. Given the long and complex history of the Greek people in the Balkans and the Mediterranean, there
are notable instances where, in one region or another, the systematic
renewal of Greek culture and even the Eastern Orthodox faith were
accomplished. Within the last twenty years there has been a great deal
of talk about the Greek Diaspora. Greeks in North America are said to
be only one more example of this centuries-long pattern. Still, in the
past Greeks lived in countries quite unlike the United States, which is
decidedly self-conscious of its own long tradition of assimilating for-
eign-born populations.

According to the 1980 census, 23,859 Greeks lived in Michigan out
of a national total of 959,856, made up of 615,882 who reported a single Greek ancestor and 343,974 who reported multiple Greek ancestors.
Interestingly, the dispersal of Greeks throughout the state has
increased rather than decreased. Of the ninety-three counties cited in
the 1980 Michigan census, Greeks were reported in all but five. Baraga,

Keweenaw, Mackinac, Ogemaw, and Tuscola were the exceptions. In 1990 the Bureau of the Census stated that out of a recorded 1,110,373 Greeks in the United States, 42,628 lived in Michigan. Many argue, and rightly so, that the U.S. Census does not recognize and so does not record third- and fourth-generation persons of Greek ancestry.

Growth and prosperity among the Greek-Americans living in Michigan is undeniable. From the first four churches that were established in Detroit, in the early decades of last century, there are now a total of eight in and immediately around the city. A grand total of twenty-two Greek Orthodox Churches are now found across Michigan. The public persona of Greeks in Michigan could not be better. Hellenic festivals, which naturally evolved out of the summer picnics, are now huge celebrations that form a much-anticipated part of summer for everyone living in Michigan.

The young second-, third-, and even fourth-generation Greek-Americans have at their disposal one of the largest Greek church facilities in the country. The Diocese Greek Orthodox Youth Camp is a one-hundred-acre site leased for ninety-nine years in Rose Hill, Michigan. Thus, predictions of the quick demise of the Greek presence in Michigan may not be as credible as some now believe.

As one writer has observed,

> [T]here had never been any doubt that our parents were more Greek than American, but as we went into the world and met other ethnics and mainstream Americans, we began to appreciate that more of their Greekness had been transferred than either of us had imagined. We had always thought of our parents as a unique generation, but our proximity to them had made us unique as well.[79]

Who can say what this unique generation and their descendants will yet accomplish?

Notes

1. Eva Catafygiotu Topping, "Michigan Philhellenes: Justice A. B. Woodward, Ypsilanti, and the Greek Revolution," *Greek Accent* 7, no. 5 (March/April 1987): 32.
2. Ibid.
3. Ibid., 33.
4. American philhellenism is masterfully presented in Stephen A. Larabee's *Hellas Observed: The American Experience of Greece, 1775–1865* (New York: New York University Press, 1957).
5. Alexander Karanikas, *Hellenes and Hellions: Modern Greek Characters in American Literature* (Urbana: University of Illinois Press, 1981), 8. See also his "Through American Eyes: Nineteenth-Century America Views Greece and Greeks," *Greek Accent* 3, no. 2 (1982).
6. Charilaos G. Lagoudakis, "Greece and Michigan," *Michigan History Magazine* 14 (1930): 23; and Pearl Kastran Ahnen, "Ypsilanti and Friends: Three Michigan Greek Communities," *Greek Accent* 5, no. 5 (March/April 1985): 5.
7. Rev. Harvey C. Colburn, *The Story of Ypsilanti* (Ypsilanti, Mich.: Ypsilanti Historical Society, 1923), 46.
8. Lagoudakis, "Greece and Michigan," 23.
9. Heike Fenton and Melvin Hecker, *The Greeks in America 1528–1977: A Chronology and Fact Book* (Dobbs Ferry, N.Y.: Oceana Publications, 1978), 4.

10. See E. P. Panagopoulos, *New Smyrna: An Eighteenth-Century Greek Odyssey* (Gainesville: University of Florida Press, 1966).

11. For other variations on this still vigorous legend see Stavros Frangos's "Legend of Legends," *GreekAmerican* (26 July 1997).

12. Theodore Saloutos, *The Greeks in the United States* (Cambridge: Harvard University Press, 1964), 45.

13. Marios Christou Stephanides, "Detroit's Greek Community," in *Ethnic Groups in the City: Culture, Institutions and Power,* ed. Otto Feinstein (Lexington, Mass.: Heath Lexington Books, 1971), 116.

14. Saloutos, *Greeks in the United States,* 45.

15. G. Saunier, *To Demotiko Tragoudi: Tis Ksenitias* (Athens: Ermes Press, 1983), 5–25.

16. *Afino Yia,* sung by Michael Kalleryis for Columbia Records in New York, cannot now be dated. As an imported record it is not listed in Richard K. Spottswood's Greek section of his *Ethnic Music on Records: A Discography of Ethnic Recordings Produced in the United States, 1893 to 1942* (Urbana: University of Illinois Press, 1990). Listening copies of this song can be found at the Grand Rapids Public Library in Grand Rapids, Michigan, and in the Greek Collection at the Marriott Library University of Utah, in Salt Lake City.

17. Columbia 7217-F/A.

18. Columbia 56327-F/B.

19. Sotiris (Sam) Chianis, "Greece: Folk Music," in *New Grove Dictionary of Music and Musicians,* ed. Stanley Sadie (London: Macmillan Publishers, 1980), 683; see also Saloutos, *Greeks in the United States,* 29–30.

20. See V. Gabrealides, "The Over-Production of Greek Currants," *Economic Journal* 5 (1895); Theodore A. Burlami, "The Overproduction of Currants: A Novel Experiment in Protection," *Economic Journal* 9 (1899); Maurice Scott Thompson, "Social and Economic Conditions of Greece," *Sociological Review* 14 (July 1913); Saloutos, *Greeks in the United States,* 29; and Janeen Arnold Costas, "The History of Migration and Political Economy of Rural Greece: A Case Study," *Journal of Modern Greek Studies* 6, no. 2 (1988).

21. Peter W. Dickson, "Pilgrim's Progress: The Tsintzinians in America," *Greek Accent* 7, no. 1 (1986); Peter W. Dickson, "Prince George and the 500 Spartans," *Greek Accent* 8, no. 2 (1987); Peter W. Dickson and Christine Warnke, "Ship of Brides," *Greek Accent* 8, no. 4 (1987); Helen Geracimos

Chaplin, "From Sparta to Spenser Street: Greek Women in Hawaii," *Hawaiian Journal of History* 13 (1979); Helen Geracimos Chaplin, "The Queen's 'Greek Artillery Fire': Greek Royalists in the Hawaiian Revolution and Counterrevolution," *Hawaiian Journal of History* 15 (1981); Helen Geracimos Chaplin, "The Greeks of Hawaii: An Odyssey from Kingdom to Statehood," *Hellenic Journal,* 17 February, 3 March, and 17 March 1983; and Helen Geracimos Chaplin, "The Greeks of Hawaii," in *New Directions in Greek American Studies,* ed. Dan Georgakas and Charles C. Moskos (New York: Pella, 1991).

22. See T. Stoianovich, "The Conquering Balkan Orthodox Merchant," *Journal of Economic History* 20 (1960); see esp. Apostolos E. Vacalopoulos, *History of Macedonia 1354–1833,* trans. Peter Megann (Thessaloniki: Institute for Balkan Studies, 1973), 387–466.

23. Mary Adams Bone, "Sault Ste. Marie: Portrait of a Parish," *Greek Accent* 3, no. 9 (May–June 1983); Marios Christou Stephanides, *The Greeks in Detroit: Authoritarianism—A Critical Analysis of Greek Culture, Personality, Attitudes, and Behavior* (San Francisco: R & E Research Associates, 1975); Ahnen, "Ypsilanti and Friends"; Stavros K. Frangos and Jane K. Cowan, *The Greek-American Family: Continuity through Change* (Washington, D.C.: National Endowment for the Humanities, Hellenic Horizons, and the Grand Rapids Public Museum, 1982); and Stavros K. Frangos, "A Survey of the Greek Communities in Michigan," Office of the Folklife Programs Report (Washington, D.C.: Smithsonian Institution, 1986).

24. Theodore Saloutos, "Greeks," in *Harvard Encyclopedia of Ethnic Groups,* ed. Stephan Thernstrom (Cambridge: Belknap, 1980), 435–36.

25. Dan Georgakas, "Hellenic Renewal or Extinction," *Greek Star,* 31 January 1991, 9.

26. Eliot G. Mears, "The Unique Position in Greek Trade of Emigrant Remittances," *Quarterly Journal of Economics* 37 (1923): 535, 540.

27. Ibid., 535.

28. "Greeks Who Stay Home," *Grand Rapids Press,* 30 October 1912.

29. Helen H. Balk, "Economic Contributions of the Greeks to the United States," *Economic Geography* 19, no. 2 (1943): 271.

30. *Detroit News,* 18 October 1912, 1; *Detroit News,* 16 October 1912, 1, 2.

31. On remittances, see Mears, "Greek Trade" and Balk, "Economic Contributions."

32. Alciviadis A. Seraphic, "The Greek Padrone System in the United States," Senate Documents, 61st Cong., 3d sess. 8 (1910–11), 392.

33. Ibid., 393.

34. Helen Zeese Papanikolas, "Toil and Rage in a New Land," *Utah Historical Quarterly* 38, no. 2 (1984).

35. Seraphic, "Padrone System," 398.

36. Ibid., 399.

37. Ibid., 398.

38. Ibid.; "The Greeks of Grand Rapids: Patriotic, Dignified, Good Boosters—Ranking with the Best People This City Contains," *Grand Rapids Press,* 1 March 1913, 10.

39. Stavros K. Frangos and Jane K. Cowan, *Grand Rapids' Greek Heritage* (Grand Rapids, Mich.: Hellenic Horizons and the National Endowment for the Humanities, 1986).

The booklet *Grand Rapids' Greek Heritage* credited to Paul Chardoul was neither written nor edited by him. The vast majority of the text presented in this booklet was drawn from the museum labels and other copy meant for the museum catalogue co-authored by Stavros K. Frangos and Jane K. Cowan. A local writer was hired to do the actual editing of the final published text.

40. See Henry Pratt Fairchild, *Greek Immigration to the United States* (New Haven, Conn.: Yale University Press, 1911); Thomas Burgess, *Greeks in America: An Account of Their Coming, Progress, Customs, Living, and Aspirations; with an Historical Introduction and the Stories of Some Famous American Greeks* (Boston: Sherman, French and Company, 1913); Thomas James Lacey, *A Study of Social Heredity as Illustrated in the Greek People* (New York: Edwin S. Gorham, 1916); J. P. Xenides, *The Greeks in America* (New York: George H. Doran Company, 1922); Saloutos, *Greeks in the United States;* Harry J. Psomiades and Alice Scourby, eds., *The Greek Community in Transition* (New York: Pella, 1982); Charles Moskos, *Greek Americans: Struggle and Success,* rev. ed. (New Brunswick, N.J.: Transaction Publishers, 1990); Dan Georgakas and Charles C. Moskos, eds., *New Directions in Greek American Studies* (New York: Pella, 1991); and Paul Koken, Theodore N. Constant, and Seraphim G. Canoutas, *A History of the Greeks in the Americas, 1453–1938* (Ann Arbor, Mich.: Proctor Publications, 1995). While Burgess does cite Michigan, and offers considerable statistical information on Greeks across the country, he is drawing directly upon Canoutas's business directory writings. See note 43 below.

41. Aside from Richard Dorson's pioneering audio fieldwork there is now only one sizeable oral history collection. Over fifty hours of oral history interviews along with more than one hundred historic photographs were collected during the 1981 National Endowment for the Humanities exhibition *The Greek-American Family: Continuity through Change,* and they are now held at the Grand Rapids Public Library. Two videos were also made during the project. For another video on the Greeks in Grand Rapids, see the film and final report written by Louis C. Murillo.

    Unfortunately a collection of much greater time span at the Wayne State University Folklore/Folklife Archive was dismantled in 1998. Selected materials were sent to the Wayne State University archives. See Philip LaRonge, *Greek and Greek-American Folklore Collections,* Annotated Holdings, List No. 5, Folklore Archive (Detroit: Wayne State University, 1982) for a survey of the original collection.

42. I am citing Burgess's *Greeks in America* (230) on the scattered communities, since his fine account is still readily available. However, a careful reading of Burgess's introduction reveals that much of the factual content of this book is derived from another contributor.

    To my dear friend . . . Seraphim G. Canoutas, L.L.B., I owe the first inspiration to write and continual assistance and encouragement throughout the labors of preparation. Nearly all the facts contained in Chapters I–V and parts of others, I took down at his dictation or translated from his book. Also he has corrected and criticized most of the manuscript. (xiii)

    From what we now know, Reverend Burgess must be referring to the various historical sections and vignettes found in, at the time of his writing, six editions of Canoutas's *Helleno-Amerikanikos Hodegos* business directories. I say this because it was not until 1918 that Canoutas first published his *O Ellenismos en Amerike, etoi Istoria tou Ellenismou en Amerike* (Hellenism in America; or the history of the Greeks in America) (New York: O Cosmos Publishing). This edition of the volume prominently featured a section in English. While it is conceivable that in 1913 Canoutas had an unpublished manuscript of his *O Ellenismos en Amerike* that Burgess was able to read, for the moment no evidence for that possibility is publicly available.

43. Burgess, *Greeks in America,* 175.

44. Canoutas's volumes were published for the most part by the New York Greek

Commercial and Information Bureau, Inc. The 1910 census report cites more Greeks in places such as Bay City, Saginaw, Detroit, and elsewhere than Canoutas lists.

45. Seraphim George Canoutas, *Helleno-Amerikanikos Hodegos: Greek American Guide and Business Directory* (New York: Hermes, 1911), 450–51.

46. Ibid.

47. RCA Victor 26-8077/A; Orthophonic S-786/A.

48. Dan Georgakas, "The Arabs among Us," *GreekAmerican* (12 March 1989), 6.

49. George Coutoumanos, "Indian Summer Imaginings," *Athene Magazine* 10, no. 1 (1949): 41.

50. Father Gregory Economiou has passed away since I last interviewed him. I am quoting from an interview with Father Economiou that was recorded on 23 October 1986. I would also like to thank Father Anastasios Gounaris, who provided me with invaluable historical documents, for his many acts of kindness.

51. See esp. "To Protest the Plan," *Grand Rapids Press,* 1 November 1909, 7.

52. Richard Dorson, "Tales of a Greek-American Family on Tape," *Fabula* 1 (1957).

53. Ibid., 115.

54. While Richard Dorson focuses exclusively on the Corombos family of Iron Mountain, he cites narratives collected among Michigan Greeks from Lansing, Marquette, and elsewhere.

55. Bone, "Sault Ste. Marie," 19.

56. Lagoudakis, "Greece and Michigan," 24–27; Albert Mayer, "Greeks," in *Ethnic Groups in Detroit: 1951* (Detroit: Wayne State University, Department of Sociology and Anthropology, 1951), 23.

57. Stephanides, "Detroit's Greek Community," 119.

58. Lagoudakis, "Greece and Michigan," 24.

59. Lois Rankin, "Detroit Nationality Groups," *Michigan History Magazine* 23, no. 2 (1939): 141.

60. Stella Politis, "Cretan Community of Detroit" (master's thesis, Wayne State University, 1967); and Stephanides, "Detroit's Greek Community."

61. Lagoudakis, "Greece and Michigan"; Rankin, "Nationality Groups"; Mayer, "Greeks"; Politis, "Cretan Community of Detroit"; Stephanides, "Detroit's Greek Community"; Marios Christou Stephanides, "Greeks and Cypriots of Detroit," *Michigan History* 56, no. 2 (1972); Stephanides, *The Greeks in*

Detroit; and Dan Georgakas, "Greektown," *GreekAmerican* (9 April 1988).

62. Libraries that hold copies of the *Athenai/The Detroit Athens* are the Library of Congress and the Franklin D. Roosevelt Library. Varying runs of *To Ethnikon Vema* from 1920 to 1955 can be found at the Detroit Public Library and the Bentley Historical Library. Later issues of *To Ethnikon Vema* from 1955 until the late 1980s can be found at the above institutions as well as the Balch Institute, Hellenic College, and the Hartford Public Library. Yet once again these are not always complete runs in any series. We should not restrict our attention to simply the ethnic press for historical and social data.

A close reading of writers such as Kotakis and Malafouris does provide biographical vignettes of Michigan Greeks. Still, the entries found in those two accounts are too episodic and individual to provide a sense of the wider community.

Church community histories exist that range from several typed pages kept in the church office for reference, to magazine-size publications marking a special event, to hardbound books commemorating some community hallmark anniversary. Examples include the Berrien County Greek Orthodox Church's photocopied handout, which is composed of two pages of "church history" along with a series of reproduced local newspaper articles, letters, and other documents that attest to that community's history, to the even more concise "Saint Demetrius Highlights and of its History," which is one paragraph long, with a chronology (see Greek Collection, Grand Rapids Public Library). An example of a full-length volume is the *Souvenir Brochure of the Dedication and Consecration of the Holy Trinity Greek Orthodox Church of Grand Rapids, Michigan.* This magazine-size publication was issued on 31 July 1955. The Grand Rapids Public Library holds not only copies of the 1955 consecration publication but also of the work titled *50th Anniversary Holy Trinity Greek Orthodox Church 1926–1976.* A selection of other such church publications is cited in the bibliography of this book.

63. See National Centre for Social Research, "Statistical Data on Greek America," *Greek American Review* 1 (spring 1976): 118.

64. Stephanides, "Greek Community," 117.

65. Rankin, " Nationality Groups," 140.

66. Ahnen, "Ypsilanti and Friends," 14.

67. Edna St. Vincent Millay, "The Greek Dance," in *Distressing Dialogues* (New York: Harper and Brother, 1924), 85–86.

68. Stoyan Christowe, "Kyotchek," *Outlook and Independent* 155, no. 2 (May 1930): 48

69. Dan Georgakas, "The Golden Age," *GreekAmerican* (10 October 1987): 6.

70. Alkis X. Xanthakis, *History of Greek Photography, 1839–1960* (Athens: Hellenic Literary and Historical Archives Society, 1988); Andre Rouille, "Exploring the World of Photography in the Nineteenth Century," in *A History of Photography: Social and Cultural Perspectives,* ed. Jean-Claude Lemagny and Andre Rouille (Cambridge: Cambridge University Press, 1986).

71. Tina Bucuvalas and Stavros Frangos, *Techne: Traditional Greek Arts in the Calumet Region* (Bloomington, Ind.: Cultural Research Associates, 1985); G. James Patterson, "Kafenia and Community: Coffee Houses and Greek Life in Aliquippa and Ambridge PA, 1938–1941," *Pittsburgh History* 74, no. 4 (1991); and Stavros K. Frangos, "Popular Greek-American Photography," *Hellenic Journal* 21, no. 25 (28 December 1995).

72. Frangos and Cowan, *Greek-American Family;* Frangos, "Popular Greek-American Photography."

73. *GreekAmerican* (7–8 April 2001): 11.

74. See *www.voithia.org.*

75. Charles C. Moskos, "Faith, Language and Culture," in *Project for Orthodox Renewal,* ed. Stephen J. Sfekas and George E. Matsouka (Chicago: Orthodox Christian Laity, 1993); Georgakas, "Arabs among Us"; Georgakas "Renewal or Extinction"; Dan Georgakas, "The America beyond Ellis Island," in *Greek American Families: Traditions and Transformations,* ed. Harry J. Psomiades, Sam J. Tsemberis, and Anna Karpathakis (New York: Pella, 1999).

76. Anna Karpathakis, "Sojourners and Permanent Settlers: Greek Immigrants of Astoria, New York" (Ph.D. diss. Columbia University, 1993), 206.

77. Constantine G. Hatzidimitriou, "Church-Community Relations in the United States," in *Greeks in English-Speaking Countries: Culture, Identity, Politics,* ed. Christos P. Ioannides (New York: Caratzas, 1997).

78. See Constance J. Tarasar, ed., *Orthodox America 1794–1976: Development of the Orthodox Church in America* (Syosset, N.Y.: Orthodox Church in America, 1975); Melton J. Gordon, "Eastern Liturgical Family," in *The Encyclopedia of American Religions,* 3d ed. (Detroit: Gale Research, 1989);

"Circuit Riders to the Slavs and Greeks: Missionary Priests and the Establishment of the Russian Orthodox Church in the American West, 1890–1910," occasional paper, Kennan Institute for Advanced Russian Studies, no. 276.

79. Dan Georgakas, "Myths about Greek Immigrants." *GreekAmerican* (27 October 1989): 5.

For Further Reference

Ahnen, Pearl Kastran. "Ypsilanti and Friends: Three Michigan Greek Communities." *Greek Accent* 5, no. 5 (March/April 1985).

———. *Legends and Legacies: The Greeks of Ann Arbor, Michigan.* Ann Arbor, Mich.: Legna Press, 1999.

Andreades, A. 1906. "The Currant Crisis in Greece." *Economic Journal* 16 (1906).

Assumption Greek Orthodox Church. *The Asssumption Family Album Commemorating the 50th Anniversary of Assumption Greek Orthodox Church.* St. Clair Shores, Mich.: Assumption Greek Orthodox Church, 1978.

Balk, Helen H. "Economic Contributions of the Greeks to the United States." *Economic Geography* 19, no. 2 (1943).

Bone, Mary Adams. "Sault Ste. Marie: Portrait of a Parish." *Greek Accent* 3, no. 9 (May–June 1983).

Bucuvalas, Tina, and Stavros Frangos. *Techne: Traditional Greek Arts in the Calumet Region.* Bloomington, Ind.: Cultural Research Associates, 1985.

Burgess, Thomas. *Greeks in America: An Account of Their Coming, Progress, Customs, Living, and Aspirations; with an Historical Introduction and the Stories of Some Famous American Greeks.* Boston: Sherman, French, and Company, 1913.

Burlami, Theodore A. "The Overproduction of Currants: A Novel Experiment in Protection." *Economic Journal* 9 (1899).

Canoutas, Seraphim George. *Helleno-Amerikanikos Hodegos: Greek American Guide and Business Directory.* New York: Hermes Press, 1911.

Chaplin, Helen Geracimos. "From Sparta to Spencer Street: Greek Women in Hawaii." *Hawaiian Journal of History* 13 (1979).

————. "The Queen's 'Greek Artillery Fire': Greek Royalists in the Hawaiian Revolution and Counterrevolution." *Hawaiian Journal of History* 15 (1981).

————. "The Greeks of Hawaii: An Odyssey from Kingdom to Statehood." *Hellenic Journal,* 17 February, 3 March, and 17 March 1983.

————. "The Greeks of Hawaii." In *New Directions in Greek American Studies,* edited by Dan Georgakas and Charles C. Moskos. New York: Pella, 1991.

Chianis, Sotiris (Sam). "Greece: Folk Music." In *New Grove Dictionary of Music and Musicians,* edited by Stanley Sadie. London: Macmillan Publishers, 1980.

Christowe, Stoyan. "Kyotchek." *Outlook and Independent* 155, no. 2 (May 1930).

Colburn, Harvey C. *The Story of Ypsilanti.* Ypsilanti, Mich.: Ypsilanti Historical Society, 1923.

Costas, Janeen Arnold. "The History of Migration and Political Economy of Rural Greece: A Case Study." *Journal of Modern Greek Studies* 6, no. 2 (1988).

Counelis, James S. "Greek Orthodox Church Statistics of the United States 1949–1989: Some Ecclesial and Social Patterns." *Journal of the Hellenic Diaspora* 16, nos. 1–4 (1989).

Coutoumanos, George. "Indian Summer Imaginings." *Athene Magazine* 10, no. 1 (1949): 41.

Dickson, Peter W. "Pilgrim's Progress: The Tsintzinians in America." *Greek Accent* 7, no. 1 (1986).

————. "Prince George and the 500 Spartans." *Greek Accent* 8, no. 2 (1987).

————. "The Greek Pilgrims: Tsakonas and Tsintzinians." In *New Directions in Greek American Studies,* edited by Dan Georgakas and Charles C. Moskos. New York: Pella, 1991.

Dickson, Peter W., and Christine Warnke. "Ship of Brides." *Greek Accent* 8, no. 4 (1987).

Dorson, Richard. "Tales of a Greek-American Family on Tape." *Fabula* 1 (1957).

Evangelismos Greek Orthodox Church. *Jubilee Book.* Detroit: Evangelismos Greek Orthodox Church, 1962.

Fairchild, Henry Pratt. *Greek Immigration to the United States.* New Haven, Conn.: Yale University Press, 1911.

Fenton, Heike, and Melvin Hecker. *The Greeks in America 1528–1977: A Chronology and Fact Book.* Dobbs Ferry, N.Y.: Oceana, 1978.

Frangos, Stavros K. "A Survey of the Greek Communities in Michigan." Office of the Folklife Programs Report. Washington, D.C.: Smithsonian Institution, 1986.

———. "Large Record Collectors: The Unrecognized Authorities." *Resound* 10, no. 2 (1991).

———. "Popular Greek-American Photography." *Hellenic Journal* 21, no. 25 (28 December 1995).

———. "Legend of Legends" *GreekAmerica* 12, no. 30 (6 July 1997).

———. "Detroit's Greektown." *National Herald* 1, no. 2 (2–3 September 2000).

———. "Snapshots of Family and Friends." *Greek-American Review,* May 2001.

Frangos, Stavros K., and Jane K. Cowan. *The Greek-American Family: Continuity through Change.* Washington, D.C.: National Endowment for the Humanities, Hellenic Horizons, and the Grand Rapids Public Museum, 1982.

———. *Grand Rapids' Greek Heritage.* Grand Rapids, Mich.: Hellenic Horizons and the National Endowment for the Humanities. 1986.

Gabrealides, V. "The Over-Production of Greek Currants." *Economic Journal* 5 (1895).

Georgakas, Dan. "The Golden Age." *GreekAmerican* (October 10, 1987).

———. "Greektown." *GreekAmerican* (9 April 1988).

———. "The Arabs among Us." *GreekAmerican* (March 12, 1989).

———. "Myths about Greek Immigrants." *GreekAmerican* (October 27, 1989).

———. "Hellenic Renewal or Extinction." *Greek Star,* January 31, 1991.

———. "The America beyond Ellis Island. In *Greek American Families: Traditions and Transformations,* edited by Harry J. Psomiades, Sam J. Tsemberis, and Anna Karpathakis. New York: Pella, 1999.

Georgakas, Dan, and Charles C. Moskos, eds. *New Directions in Greek American Studies.* New York: Pella, 1991.

Gordon, Melton J. "Eastern Liturgical Family." In *The Encyclopedia of American Religions.* 3d ed. Detroit: Gale Research, 1989.

Hatzidimitriou, Constantine G. "Church-Community Relations in the United States." In *Greeks in English-Speaking Countries: Culture, Identity, Politics,* edited by Christos P. Ioannides. New York: Caratzas Press, 1997.

Hodge, Lyman F. *Photius Fisk: A Bibliography.* Boston, 1891.

Karanikas, Alexander. *Hellenes and Hellions: Modern Greek Characters in American Literature.* Urbana: University of Illinois Press, 1981.

———. "Through American Eyes: Nineteenth-Century America Views Greece and Greeks. " *Greek Accent* 3, no. 2 (1982).

Kardaras, Basil P. "A Study of the Martial and Familial Options of the Second-Generation Greek-Americans in the Detroit Metropolitan Area." Master's thesis, Wayne State University, 1977.

Karpathakis, Anna. "Sojourners and Permanent Settlers: Greek Immigrants of Astoria, New York." Ph.D. diss., Columbia University, 1993.

———. "Whose Church Is It Anyway? Greek Immigrants of Astoria, New York, and their Church." *Journal of the Hellenic Diaspora* 20, no. 1 (1994).

Kopan, Andrew T. *Education and Greek Immigrants in Chicago 1892–1973: A Study in Ethnic Survival.* New York: Garland Publishing Company, 1990.

Kotakis, Spyridonos P. *Hoi Hellenes en Amerike.* Chicago: S. P. Kotakis Printing Press, 1908.

Kyrou, Alexandros K., and Stavros K. Frangos. "Diaspora Studies: Hellenic Diaspora." In *Greece in Modern Times. An Annotated Bibliography, Volume 1,* edited by Stratos E. Constantinidis. Lanham, Md.: Scarecrow Press, 1990.

Lacey, Thomas James. *A Study of Social Heredity as Illustrated in the Greek People.* New York: Edwin S. Gorham, 1916.

Lagoudakis. Charilaos G. "Greece and Michigan." *Michigan History Magazine* 14 (1930).

Larabee, Stephen A. *Hellas Observed: The American Experience of Greece, 1775–1865.* New York: New York University Press, 1957.

LaRonge, Philip. *Greek and Greek-American Folklore Collections.* Annotated Holdings, List No. 5. Folklore Archive. Detroit: Wayne State University, 1982.

Loucopoulos, Eugenios. *Dedication Book of the Saint George Greek Orthodox Church.* Sault Saint Marie: Saint George Greek Orthodox Church, 1958.

Malafouris, Bobbi. *Ellines tis Amerikis, 1528–1948.* New York: no publisher, 1948.

———. "The Struggle for a Living." *Journal of the Hellenic Diaspora* 14 (1987).

Mayer, Albert. "Greeks." In *Ethnic Groups in Detroit: 1951.* Detroit: Wayne State University, Department of Sociology and Anthropology, 1951.

Mears, Eliot G. "The Unique Position in Greek Trade of Emigrant Remittances." *Quarterly Journal of Economics* 37 (1923).

Melton, J. Gordon. "Eastern Liturgical Family." In *The Encyclopedia of American Religions.* 3d ed. Detroit: Gale Research, 1989.

Millay, Edna St. Vincent. "The Greek Dance." In *Distressing Dialogues.* New York: Harper and Brother, 1924.

Moskos. Charles C. *Greek Americans: Struggle and Success.* Rev. ed. New Brunswick, N.J.: Transaction Publishers, 1990.

———. "Faith, Language and Culture." In *Project for Orthodox Renewal,* edited by Stephen J. Sfekas and George E. Matsouka. Chicago: Orthodox Christian Laity, 1993.

Murillo, Louis C. "Greek-Americans in Grand Rapids." Ethnic Heritage Studies Project, Grand Rapids Junior College, 1978–79.

National Centre for Social Research. "Statistical Data on Greek America." *Greek American Review* 1 (spring 1976).

Panagopoulos, E. P. *New Smyrna: An Eighteenth-Century Greek Odyssey.* Gainesville: University of Florida Press, 1966.

Papanikolas, Helen Zeese. "Toil and Rage in a New Land." *Utah Historical Quarterly* 38, no. 2 (1984).

Papazoglou, Ourania. "Greek Town Detroit: Fortress under Siege." *Greek Accent* 1, no. 8 (March 1981).

Patterson, G. James. "Kafenia and Community: Coffee Houses and Greek Life in Aliquippa and Ambridge PA, 1938–1941." *Pittsburgh History* 74, no. 4 (winter 1991).

Peck, Gunther. *Reinventing Free Labor: Padrones and Immigrant Workers in the North American West, 1880–1930.* Cambridge: Cambridge University Press, 2000.

Politis, Stella. "Cretan Community of Detroit." Master's thesis, Wayne State University, 1967.

Preketes, Charles. "The History of the Greek Community of Ann Arbor." In *St. Nicholas Greek Orthodox Church of Ann Arbor, Michigan.* Ann Arbor, Mich.: St. Nicholas Greek Orthodox Church, 1945.

Psomiades, Harry J., and Alice Scourby. *The Greek Community in Transition.* New York: Pella, 1982.

Rankin, Lois. "Detroit Nationality Groups." *Michigan History Magazine* 23, no. 2 (1939).

Rouille, Andre. "Exploring the World of Photography in the Nineteenth Century." In *A History of Photography: Social and Cultural Perspectives,* edited by Jean-Claude Lemagny and Andre Rouille. Cambridge: Cambridge University Press, 1986.

St. Nicholas Greek Orthodox Church. *Consecration.* Troy, Mich.: St. Nicholas
    Greek Orthodox Church, 19 May 1996.

Saloutos, Theodore. *The Greeks in the United States.* Cambridge: Harvard
    University Press, 1964.

———. "Causes and Patterns of Greek Emigration to the United States."
    Perspectives in American History 7 (1973).

———. "Greeks." In *Harvard Encyclopedia of Ethnic Groups,* edited by Stephan
    Thernstrom. Cambridge: Belknap Press of Harvard University, 1980.

Saunier, G. *To Demotiko Tragoudi: Tis Ksenitias.* Athens: Ermes Press, 1983.

Seraphic, Alciviadis A. "The Greek Padrone System in the United States." Senate
    Documents. 61st Cong., 3d sess., 8 (1911).

Smoak, Janet M. Everts. *Guide to the Greek Collections in the Manuscripts
    Division, Marriott Library, Special Collections, University of Utah.* Salt Lake
    City: University of Utah, 1922.

Spottswood, Richard K. *Ethnic Music on Records: A Discography of Ethnic
    Recordings Produced in the United States, 1893 to 1942.* Urbana: University
    of Illinois Press, 1990.

Stephanides, Marios Christou. "Detroit's Greek Community." In *Ethnic Groups in
    the City: Culture, Institutions and Power,* edited by Otto Feinstein.
    Lexington, Mass.: Heath Lexington Books, 1971.

———. "Greeks and Cypriots of Detroit." *Michigan History* 56, no. 2 (1972).

———. *The Greeks in Detroit: Authoritarianism—A Critical Analysis of Greek
    Culture, Personality, Attitudes, and Behavior.* San Francisco: R & E Research
    Associates, 1975.

Stoianovich, T. "The Conquering Balkan Orthodox Merchant." *Journal of
    Economic History* 20 (1960).

Tarasar, Constance J., ed. *Orthodox America 1794–1976: Development of the Ortho-
    dox Church in America.* Syosset, N.Y.: Orthodox Church in America, 1975.

Thompson, Maurice Scott. "Social and Economic Conditions of Greece." *Socio-
    logical Review* 14 (July 1913).

Topping, Eva Catafygiotu. "Judge Woodward: Godfather of Ypsilanti." In *Clergy-
    Laity Congress Album (Detroit).* New York: Greek Orthodox Archdiocese
    Press, 1978.

———. "Philhellenes in Michigan." *Michigan History* 65, no. 2 (1981).

———. "Michigan Philhellenes: Judge A. B. Woodward, Ypsilanti, and the Greek
    Revolution." *Greek Accent* 7, no. 5 (March/April 1987).

Tselos, George. "Archival Sources for the History of the Greek-American Community: Problems and Challenges." *Journal of the Hellenic Diaspora* 16, no. 1–4 (1989).

Vacalopoulos, Apostolos E. *History of Macedonia 1354–1833.* Translated by Peter Megann. Thessaloniki: Institute for Balkan Studies, 1973.

Vyronis Jr., Speros. *A Brief History of the Greek-American Community of St. George, Memphis, Tennessee, 1962–1982.* Malibu, Calif.: Undena, 1982.

Xanthakis, Alkis X. *History of Greek Photography 1839–1960.* Athens: Hellenic Literary and Historical Archives Society, 1988.

Xenakis, John. "A Short History of the Assumption Church." In *35th Anniversary Souvenir Album.* Detroit: Assumption Greek Orthodox Church, 1963.

Xenides, Rev. J. P. *The Greeks in America.* New York: George H. Doran, 1922.

Zenelis, John. "A Bibliographic Guide on Greek Americans." In *The Greek Community in Transition,* edited by Harry J. Psomiades and Alice Scourby. New York: Pella, 1982.

Index